"The story of Philip Malloy, his family, friends, teachers, and school shouts to be shared."

So said the *New York Times* in reviewing Avi's award-winning documentary novel *Nothing But the Truth*. The play by Ronn Smith, based on the Avi novel, is Philip Malloy's story—a dramatic tale of a student who broke a faculty rule, was suspended from school, and found that he and his family were soon caught up in a national media event, trading charges and countercharges regarding respect, freedom, and patriotism.

Avon Books by
AVI

THE BARN
BLUE HERON
THE MAN WHO WAS POE
NOTHING BUT THE TRUTH
A PLACE CALLED UGLY
POPPY
PUNCH WITH JUDY
ROMEO AND JULIET—TOGETHER (AND ALIVE!) AT LAST
SOMETHING UPSTAIRS
SOMETIMES I THINK I HEAR MY NAME
S.O.R. LOSERS
THE TRUE CONFESSIONS OF CHARLOTTE DOYLE
"WHO WAS THAT MASKED MAN, ANYWAY?"
WINDCATCHER

Coming Soon

TOM, BABETTE, & SIMON:
THREE TALES OF TRANSFORMATION

NOTHING BUT THE TRUTH

A Play by
RONN SMITH
based on the award-winning novel by

AVI

AN AVON FLARE BOOK

NOTHING BUT THE TRUTH is an original publication of Avon Books. This work has never before appeared in book form.

Play production rights are retained by Ronn Smith c/o McIntosh & Otis, 310 Madison Avenue, New York, New York 10017.

AVON BOOKS
A division of
The Hearst Corporation
1350 Avenue of the Americas
New York, New York 10019

Copyright © 1997 by Ronn Smith
Original introduction by Avi copyright © 1997 by Avi
Published by arrangement with the author
Library of Congress Catalog Card Number: 96-97042
ISBN: 0-380-78715-6

First Avon Flare Printing: March 1997

AVON FLARE TRADEMARK REG. U.S. PAT. OFF. AND IN OTHER COUNTRIES, MARCA REGISTRADA, HECHO EN U.S.A.

Printed in the U.S.A.

RA 10 9 8 7 6 5 4 3 2 1

For Jordan, Brenna, Meghan, and Zachary

INTRODUCTION

by Avi

In its original form my novel, *Nothing But the Truth*, told a story with the use of notes, dialogues, memos, newspaper articles, and diary entries. Each item was dated and timed so as to create a gripping story.

I wrote it that way in order to take my author's voice, so to speak, out of the story, wanting, instead, to put the reader in charge. That way readers could experience just how complicated that thing is we call truth. The novel became a kind of mystery story—not a "who done it," so much as a "what happened?"

The form of *Nothing But the Truth* was new to many people. Though the book is a novel, albeit, a "documentary novel," as I called it, a fair number of people who enjoyed the book called it a play when writing to me.

Actually there were a couple of literary creations that helped me create the form. The first *was* a play, but a particular kind. Let me explain.

When I first began to write—back in high school and college—I wanted to write plays. In my studies of drama, I came upon a type of play called a "living newspaper."

Living newspapers—written and produced in the nineteen-thirties—were teaching plays. That is, they attempted to teach audiences about the day's politics and economics. While they did have plots and characters, they also called for the projection of documents on screens, had actors read other documents and newspaper stories, and even shared statistics with audiences. In short, they dramatized current politics.

While I never saw one of these plays, I did read them and found the form fascinating. In fact, in college I tried to write a living newspaper. What was it about? How hard college was! I hasten to say it was never staged. But I did remember the form.

The other thing that really helped me shape my idea for the novel, *Nothing But the Truth*, also came from the nineteen-thirties. At that time a kind of mystery game was put on the market. It came in a box, and consisted of a collection of documents which constituted the evidence pertaining to a murder investigation. There were police reports, photographs, memos, interviews, tickets, train schedules, and even (as I recall) a cigarette stub and match. You sifted (and read) all these bits of evidence to determine who the criminal was. Then you opened a sealed envelope to see if you were right.

Thirty years later this same game was put on the market again, not in a box, but as a *book*. That is, the publisher put the "evidence" in regular book form, with illustrations of the cigarette stub, tickets, etc. Now the reader had to read a *book* of evidence to solve the mystery.

In legal language, evidence is called "discovery." The first title of *Nothing But the Truth* was just that: *Discovery*.

So it was a play and a game—both of which I experienced as *books*—that gave me the idea for the form of *Nothing But the Truth*.

Since the novel was published many schools have requested permission to do it as a play. Having put play-writing far behind me, I turned to my friend Ronn Smith, a skilled playwright, to write a good theatrical version—which he has done. This version of *Nothing But the Truth* is truly a play. In fact, it might be interesting to compare the play version to the original novel. You'll see there's quite a difference.

In some respects, what you have in your hands is the kind of play I was trying to write more than thirty years ago. Here's hoping it gets performed on a stage many times.

Avi
Boulder, Colorado

FOREWORD

by Ronn Smith

I have been involved in theatre for many years. I have directed new plays by young playwrights, served as a dramaturg (something of a research assistant) for established directors, and written about the theatre and its designers. And naturally I am an avid theatre-goer.

What I have learned from the people I have worked with, the designers I have interviewed, and the productions I have seen is deceptively simple. Whether it is a Greek tragedy or a Shakespearean comedy or a play by Tennessee Williams, the single most important component for good theatre is a good story. This is not to say that the other elements of theatre—i.e., acting, direction, scenery, lighting, costumes—are not important. But for me, the most satisfying theatrical experiences I have had were those that involved a good story.

Avi's novel, *Nothing But the Truth*, is a good story. I don't know if it is a true story that actually happened somewhere that one could point to on a map, but it feels true. And I like the way it is told. The juxtaposition of dialogue, diary entries, letters, and memos (to mention only some of the literary devices used by Avi) does present, as Avi writes in his introduction, "a kind of mystery story—not a 'who done it?' so much as a 'what happened?'" story.

When Avi asked me to adapt his novel to the stage, I knew that I would have to simplify the story. One of the wonderful things about novels in general and mystery novels in particular is that the reader—if she or he chooses to—can flip forward to get some idea about where the story is going, or turn back to a previous page to check on a detail. This is very helpful when it comes to trying to solve a mystery before reaching the end of the book.

In the theatre, however, such flipping back and forth is impossible (although on several occasions in the theatre I have been tempted to stand up and shout, "Hey, that was really good; let's see that part again!"). The experience one has while watching theatre is more linear, which necessitates that the story must be told in a simple, more straightforward fashion. This is especially necessary if the audience's attention is not to wander during the performance.

If you compare this script and Avi's novel, you will discover that I have downplayed or eliminated certain parts of the story. This is not because they are less important than other parts, but because I could not fit all of Avi's rich, wonderful detail on the stage in a reasonable period of time. I have, however, tried to retain the "what happened?" mystery of the novel, which I think is the key to the novel's great appeal. Even at the end, as the light fades on Philip Malloy, it is difficult to say precisely who was right or who was wrong or exactly what happened. If, on leaving the theatre after the performance, the audience is heard discussing these questions, then you will know that the story has been told properly and that the production was a success.

Ronn Smith
Providence, Rhode Island

CHARACTERS
(in order of appearance)

Philip Malloy, student (14 years old)
Margaret Narwin, teacher (mid to late 50s)
Bernard Lunser, teacher
Dr. Gertrude Doane, principal
Student #1
Student #2
Student #3
Allison Doresett, student
Coach Earl Jamison, teacher
Ben Malloy, Philip's father
Susan Malloy, Philip's mother
Ken Barchet, student
Lisa Gibbons, student
Jacob Benison, teacher
Todd Becker, student
Janet Barsky, student
Dr. Joseph Palleni, assistant principal
Ted Griffen, school board candidate
Jennifer Stewart, reporter for the *Manchester Record*
Dr. Albert Seymour, school superintendent
Jake Barlow, talk radio host
Mrs. Gloria Harland, chairperson of school board
Caller #1 (Steve)
Caller #2 (Liz)
Robert Duval, reporter for the *St. Louis Post-Dispatch*

Caller #3 (Roger)
Cynthia Gambia, student
Jessica Wittington
Hank Morgan
Charles Elderson
Carlton Haven
David Maik
Laura Jacobs
Rolando Merchaud
Ms. Harbor
American Legionnaire
George Brookover, principal of Washington
Academy
Miss Rooney, teacher at Washington Academy

PLACE

Almost anywhere in the United States.

TIME

The present.

Production Notes

The stage is divided into four main acting areas: up-stage center (UC), stage left (SL), stage right (SR), and downstage center (DC). Platforms are used to define these four primary acting areas, with the UC platform being the highest and the DC platform—the area closest to the audience—the lowest. The SL and SR platforms are of equal height. Two additional acting areas, downstage left and downstage right, can be used for some of the telephone calls and short monologues.

The UC acting area is used for the Malloy household; it contains a kitchen table and three chairs. The SL acting area is used for various public or student-affiliated locations in the high school; it contains four or five student desks and maybe a row of lockers set so as not to obscure the UC acting area. The SR acting area is used for several administrative offices; it contains a single, solid desk and a desk chair. The DC acting area is a neutral space used for miscellaneous locations; it contains no furniture or other items.

A large rear projection screen is positioned behind each of the SR, UC, and SL acting areas. If production resources are limited, then one rear projection screen behind the UC acting area will suffice. When slides of classrooms, hallways, and offices are used to help "set the scene," these images are of a school near the theatre or, when the play is being produced by or in a school, of the school itself. (If production resources are severely limited, these screens and the projection of slides can be eliminated entirely. The absence of projected images will not adversely affect the production.)

Because the action of the play takes place in many short scenes in many different locations, it is recommended that the physical elements of the production be kept as simple as possible. The use of heavy or awkward set pieces should be kept to a minimum and props restricted to those the actors can carry on and off stage themselves. In this way, the production always remains focused on the characters and the story they are telling—never on how the story is being told.

Blackouts, except where indicated in the script, are to be avoided throughout the entire performance. At the end of each scene, the actors freeze in position for a quick beat, after which they move into position for the following scene. As the actors move to their new positions, the lighting should change to help indicate a new scene in another location.

Scene titles are to be projected either on one of the rear projection screens or on a screen suspended over the stage (or maybe just beneath the proscenium arch). Exactly how and when the actors, lighting, and scene titles change must be choreographed carefully so that all changes are smooth, quick, and consistent throughout the production.

An Additional Note

Although the list of characters indicates that there are thirty-eight speaking roles, the play can be performed by as few as ten actors (five male and five female). When ten actors are used, the roles should be assigned in the following manner:

Male

Actor #1:   Philip Malloy
Actor #2:   Student #1, Ken Barchet, Todd Becker
Actor #3:   Bernard Lunser, Jacob Benison, Ted Griffen, Caller #1 (Steve), Robert Duval, Hank Morgan, Carlton Haven, George Brookover

Actor #4:   Coach Earl Jamison, Dr. Joseph Palleni,
            Jake Barlow, Charles Elderson, David
            Maik, American Legionnaire
Actor #5:   Ben Malloy, Dr. Albert Seymour, Caller
            #3 (Roger), Rolando Merchaud.

Female

Actor #6:   Student #2, Allison Doresett
Actor #7:   Student #3, Lisa Gibbons, Janet Barsky,
            Cynthia Gambia
Actor #8:   Margaret Narwin
Actor #9:   Dr. Gertrude Doane, Mrs. Gloria Harland,
            Caller #2 (Liz), Miss Rooney
Actor #10: Susan Malloy, Jennifer Stewart, Jessica
            Wittington, Laura Jacobs, Ms. Harbor

The following "memo" should be distributed to all audience members as they enter the theatre, or may be included as part of the program:

MEMO

HARRISON SCHOOL DISTRICT

Where Our Children Are Educated, Not Just Taught

Dr. Albert Seymour   Mrs. Gloria Harland
Superintendent   *Chairman, School Board*

STANDARD FORMAT FOR
MORNING ANNOUNCEMENTS ON
PUBLIC-ADDRESS SYSTEM

1. 8:05 A.M. The Principal, or in his stead the Assistant Principal, or in his stead a designated member of the faculty, will say, "Good morning to all students, faculty, and staff. Today is Monday (or whatever day), January (or whatever month) 3 (or whatever day). Today will be a Schedule A (or B) day" (depending on what schedule).

2. Say, "Today in history . . ." (Please consult *Book of Days* in Principal's office for appropriate references. Limit is three items.)

3. Say, "Please all rise and stand at respectful, silent attention for the playing of our national anthem."

4. Turn on tape of anthem.

5. After anthem is complete, say, "I have these announcements." All administration and faculty announcements shall be made at this point.

6. Say, "May I now introduce⎯⎯⎯⎯⎯⎯⎯⎯ (name of student, grade) for today's sport and club news. Have a good day."

7. Student announcements.

8. All announcements should end by 8:15 latest.

Dr. Joseph Palleni
Assistant Principal

The following "article" should be distributed during the intermission:

SUSPENDED FOR PATRIOTISM
by J. Stewart, Education Reporter

Harrison. While it may appear to be an April Fools' Day joke, tenth-grader Philip Malloy of Harrison High School was suspended for singing The Star-Spangled Banner.

His parents, Susan and Benjamin Malloy of Harrison Township, do not consider themselves super-patriotic, but they did raise their son to have pride in our country. It was only natural then for Philip to sing along when the national anthem was played on tape during the morning exercises. According to Harrison School superintendent Dr. A. Seymour, there is no rule against singing the anthem. Indeed, in every other class Philip did just that. His new homeroom teacher, Ms. Margaret Narwin, however, changed the rules. Every time Philip lifted his voice to sing she threw him out of class, insisting a disturbance was being created.

School principal Dr. Gertrude Doane, who admits that the student has no previous bad marks on his record, saw the issue only as one of discipline, and referred all questions regarding school policy to Dr. Joseph Palleni, assistant principal. Dr. Palleni, however, refused to be interviewed regarding the incident.

ACT ONE

PROLOG

*Spot up on PHILIP MALLOY, who is standing
in the DC acting area.*

PHILIP MALLOY (*to the audience*): Two questions. Do you swear to tell the truth, the whole
truth, and nothing but the truth? (*pause*) Does
anyone ever say no?

Blackout.

SCENE ONE

SLIDE: "Tuesday, March 13. 10:35 P.M. From the
         Diary of Philip Malloy"

*Lights up on PHILIP MALLOY, standing in the
DC acting area. He is holding his diary.*

PHILIP MALLOY (*to the audience*): Coach Jamison stopped me in the hall today to say that I
should try out for the track team! That with me
on the Harrison High team we could be county
champs. Fantastic! He wouldn't say that unless
he meant it. Will have to ask the folks to help

3

me get new shoes. But Dad was so excited I'm sure he'll help. (*He begins to leave, but then stops and turns back to the audience.*)

Oh, yeah. Sarah Gloss came over at lunch to say this girl, Allison Doresett, likes me. I wasn't sure who Allison was. Then I remembered. She's in my English class. Bet she heard about my running. Girls like guys who win. Ta-da! It's Malloy Magic time!

Talk about Malloy Magic. This time for—da-dum!—Miss Narwin. I mean, what can you do with an English teacher who's so uptight she must have been put together with superglue. She won't let people have their own minds about anything! And the stuff she makes us read! I can't believe how *boring* Jack London is! *The Call of the Wild*. Talk about dogs! Ma says *she* had to read it in school. There has to be better stuff to read. I thought high school was going to be different. (*beat*) Have to figure out a way to run past Narwin.

SLIDE: "10:45 P.M. From a Letter Written by Margaret Narwin to Her Sister, Anita Wigham"

PHILIP MALLOY exits and MARGARET NARWIN, holding the letter, enters. She stops in the DC acting area.

MARGARET NARWIN (*to the audience*): Yes, a body gets a little tired after doing *anything* for twenty-one years. And I have been teaching at Harrison High for that long. But I still believe I was meant to bring fine literature to young

4

minds. When the connection is made—and from time to time it *is* made—it's all worth it. The truth is, I like my work. (*beat*)

But the other truth, Anita, is that students today are not what they used to be. There is no love of literature. They come to it reluctantly, fighting every inch of the way. I like them and their capacity for independence, but they seem to lack caring for anything other than themselves. If they ask me once more "What's this have to do with *us*?" I think I'll scream.

For example, right now I'm teaching *The Call of the Wild*. This boy, Philip Malloy, raised his hand to say he didn't understand "who was calling who." Now if I were to laugh, he would have been insulted. And I would have lost him. You have to treat students with such care and fairness.

This Philip is only a middling student, which is a shame. He's a nice-looking boy. Intelligent. With real potential. Perhaps that's why he irritates me so, for he shows no desire to strive, to make sacrifices for the betterment of himself. Like so many students, he exhibits *no* desire to learn. But it's not even *that* that I mind so much. It's a certain something—a resistance—to the idea that literature is important. But it is. I know it is. If I could only convince students of this.

I can hear you saying, "Come down to Florida." Anita, I don't know if I am ready. Yes, I could take early retirement, but the truth is, I would be lost without my books, my teaching, my students.

SCENE TWO

SLIDE: "Thursday, March 15. 8:05 A.M. Bernard
　　　Lunser's Homeroom Class"

*PHILIP MALLOY, STUDENT #1, STUDENT
#2, STUDENT #3, and BERNARD LUNSER
in SL acting area. General commotion. SLIDE
(on rear projection screen behind SL area):
Classroom wall, maybe a blackboard or a row of
windows.*

BERNARD LUNSER: Let's go! Let's go! Time to
grab the moment!

INTERCOM (*voice of DR. GERTRUDE DOANE*):
Good morning to all students, faculty, and staff.
Today is Thursday, March fifteenth. Today will
be a Schedule A day.

BERNARD LUNSER: Get that, bozos? *A* day!

INTERCOM: Today in history. On this day in
forty-four B.C., Julius Caesar was assassinated.

BERNARD LUNSER: And right after that they all
ate a Caesar salad.

INTERCOM: It was in eighteen-twenty that Maine was admitted to the United States.

BERNARD LUNSER: And by eighteen-twenty-one they wanted out.

INTERCOM: Please all rise and stand at respectful, silent attention for the playing of our national anthem.

PHILIP MALLOY and the other STUDENTS stand. PHILIP MALLOY's attention is on the book lying open on his desk as the first verse of The Star-Spangled Banner *is played over the intercom. (In following scenes, unless otherwise noted, fade out music soon after the dialogue has been concluded.)*

Oh, say, can you see by the dawn's early light,
What so proudly we hailed at the twilight's last gleaming? . . .

BERNARD LUNSER: Okay, Philip, is that your homework you're working on?

Whose broad stripes and bright stars, thro' the perilous fight . . .

PHILIP MALLOY: I'm trying to pass an exam.

BERNARD LUNSER: Ah, the famous wit and wisdom of Mr. Malloy. Put the book away.

O'er the ramparts we watched were so gallantly stream-
ing? . . .

PHILIP MALLOY: Just one last paragraph?

BERNARD LUNSER: Away, Philip! Or I'll make
you sing a solo!

And the rockets' red glare, the bombs bursting in air,
Gave proof thro' the night that our flag was still there.
Oh, say does that star-spangled banner yet wave
O'er the land of the free and the home of the brave?

SLIDE: "11:05 P.M. From the Diary of Philip Malloy"

PHILIP MALLOY in the DC acting area. He is
holding his diary.

PHILIP MALLOY (*to the audience*): Winter term
exams next week. I hate them. Studying is so boring! Three exams scheduled in one day! The trick
is getting past the teacher. It's like a race. You
have to have a strategy, know when to take it
easy, when to turn on the juice. Get teachers to
think you're in control. Or when all else fails,
make them laugh.

The exam I really want to study for is math.
People think I'm weird, but I like math. I won't
waste time on English. What can you say about
a dog? Besides, it's just a matter of opinion! If
only I could get Narwin to crack a smile. (*beat*)

Been checking out Allison. She looked cool today. Dad says that girls really go for sports stars.

8

Sunny at first today. Then cloudy. Bit of rain. Then sunny again. Still, I got in a workout. Mostly wind sprints. Then twenty minutes on Dad's rowing machine. Track team practice starts next week. Can't wait. That's all Dad and I talk about.

SCENE THREE

SLIDE: "Friday, March 16. Memo to Philip from Dr. Joseph Palleni, Assistant Principal"

PHILIP MALLOY in SL acting area. He is holding the memo. SLIDE: School hallway.

PHILIP MALLOY (*reading*): "Dear Philip. As we head into spring term, the faculty committee has made some changes in homeroom assignments. This will facilitate the movements of students, as well as allow for a greater degree of freedom in the planning of spring term extracurricular schedules. Your new homeroom teacher is Miss Narwin, in room two-oh-six. Effective Wednesday, March twenty-eight. Thank you for your co-operation."

PHILIP MALLOY looks up at the audience, a look of horror on his face.

SLIDE: "8:20 P.M. Telephone Conversation between Philip and Allison Doresett"

PHILIP MALLOY in the UC acting area. ALLISON DORESETT in DC acting area. SLIDE

10

(on rear projection screen behind UC area): Kitchen wall in the Malloy household.

PHILIP MALLOY: Can I speak to Allison, please?

ALLISON DORESETT: This is she.

PHILIP MALLOY: Oh, Allison. Hi, this is Phil Malloy.

ALLISON DORESETT: Oh, hi.

PHILIP MALLOY: Hey, I . . . I was wondering . . . the English exam. Did you read *The Call of the Wild* yet?

ALLISON DORESETT: I finished it last night. We're supposed to review it tomorrow for the exam.

PHILIP MALLOY: I lost my copy.

ALLISON DORESETT: You what?

PHILIP MALLOY: It wasn't my fault. See, I had this idea . . . I thought I'd read it to a dog.

ALLISON DORESETT: A dog!

PHILIP MALLOY: Well, it's about dogs, right? So I started to read it to him . . . this really mean dog . . . slobbering mouth, running eyes, the whole bit. Only, see, he grabs it and starts to run away.

ALLISON DORESETT (*laughing*): This isn't true . . .

PHILIP MALLOY: No, listen! I'm serious! And I chased him into a yard and there he was . . . burying the book in the ground. I couldn't get it back. My point is, *he* hated it too!

ALLISON DORESETT: You're too much. I dare you to tell that to Narwin.

PHILIP MALLOY: You think I should?

ALLISON DORESETT: You always make remarks.

PHILIP MALLOY: Somebody's got to keep the class awake.

ALLISON DORESETT: I hate to tell you, Phil, but I liked the book.

PHILIP MALLOY: Whoops! Sorry, wrong number! Bye!

SCENE FOUR

SLIDE: "Monday, March 19. Margaret Narwin's
Winter Term Exam"

*PHILIP MALLOY and MARGARET NAR-
WIN in the SL acting area, facing the audience.
They are each holding a copy of the exam.
SLIDE: classroom wall (this image is not the
same as the one used in Scene Two, but should
be used for all subsequent scenes that take place
in Margaret Narwin's classroom).*

PHILIP MALLOY (*to the audience*): "Question
four: What is the significance of Jack London's
choice in making Buck, the dog in *The Call of the
Wild*, the focus of the novel? Is the dog meant to
be symbolic? Explain your answer. Can *people*
learn from this portrayal of a dog? Expand on
these ideas."

MARGARET NARWIN (*incredulous, reading
Philip Malloy's answer*): "The significance of Buck
in Jack London's *The Call of the Wild* is that Buck
is symbolic of a cat. You might think that cats
have nothing to do with the book, but *that* is the
point. Dogs are willing to sit around and have
writers write about them, which, in my personal

13

opinion, makes them dumb. I think cats are smart. Cats don't like cold. A book that takes up so much time about a dog is pretty dumb. The book itself is a dog. That is what people learn from Jack London's *The Call of the Wild*."

PHILIP MALLOY (*reading Margaret Narwin's response*): "Philip, this is an unacceptable response. *The Call of the Wild* is an acknowledged masterpiece of American literature. You are not required to like it. You *are*, however, required to give it your *respectful*, thoughtful attention. When you get your Winter term grade, consider it a warning. Exam grade: C-minus."

PHILIP MALLOY looks up at the audience, surprised.

SCENE FIVE

DR. GERTRUDE DOANE in SR acting area. She is reading the memo. SLIDE (on rear projection screen behind SR area): Office wall.

DR. GERTRUDE DOANE: "Attached please find my application for a summer grant-in-aid. I am applying to the State University for a summer program entitled, 'New Approaches to the Teaching of Literature for Today's Students.' It's an intensive two-week workshop in which university professors will present new ideas for the experienced high school English teacher. The application form requires both an approval and a recommendation from my head administrator, which is why I write you.

"I have been teaching for a long time. And I feel I am in need of new ideas, strategies, concepts to keep my teaching vital. The truth is—and I believe I can speak honestly to you about this—I feel that I am a little out of touch with the current crop of students. I want to find new works and new ways to reach them.

"In any case, you can easily see that the real beneficiaries of the program will be the students of Harrison High. I know how restricted district money is these days, but I have not asked for this kind of support before. The State University tuition, two thousand dollars, is quite beyond my personal budget. May I ask you to give this request your personal and immediate attention. Sincerely, Margaret Narwin."

SCENE SIX

SLIDE: "Friday, March 23. 10:30 P.M. From the Diary of Philip Malloy"

PHILIP MALLOY in the DC acting area. He is holding his diary.

PHILIP MALLOY (*to the audience*): Got my term grades. Math, an A. Awesome wicked. B minus in Biology. That's okay, too. And I got a C in History, which is cool. All of that stuff is dead anyway. A straight B in Health. But then I got a D in English! Narwin is so dumb she didn't get the joke. What she really wants is for us to write down the things *she* thinks. And now I'm going to get Narwin for a homeroom teacher, too. Not me.

Worked out with Mike at the track. Short sprints. Starts. Long runs. It calmed me down. Tryouts for the team are on Monday. Can't wait. I know I'll make it. Will have to ask the folks to spring for those new shoes. (*beat*)

Sarah Gloss was reading this book, *The Outsiders*. She said it was the best book she'd ever read. Said she'd loan it to me when she was done.

Saw Allison today. Did this thing. (*PHILIP MALLOY sweeps off his imaginary hat and makes a*

17

big, theatrical bow.) She cracked up. I'm getting to her.

Went out to this restaurant tonight called Treasure Island. Seafood place. Dad said I could have anything on the menu except lobster. I ordered a hamburger and fries. Dad was pretty sore. I wish people would say what they mean.

SCENE SEVEN

SLIDE: "Monday, March 26. Memo to Margaret
       Narwin from Dr. Doane"

*MARGARET NARWIN in SL acting area. She
is reading the memo. SLIDE: Classroom wall.*

MARGARET NARWIN: "As much as I would
like to be supportive of your desire to take the
'New Approaches to the Teaching of Literature'
workshop, I am afraid I cannot give it formal approval. The problem is severely limited district
money. Such funds as are available for this kind
of support have already been allocated. In fact,
the last of them just went to Kimberly Howard,
the music teacher, who will be taking a summer
course in marching band techniques . . . something that will give pleasure to so many people,
and, it is hoped, encourage greater attendance at
athletic events. (*beat*)

"I do want to say, on a personal level, how
much I admire your willingness to expand your
intellectual and teaching horizons. You have always been one of our best teachers, and I know
you will continue to be so. Sincerely, Dr. Gertrude Doane."

SLIDE: "11:20 A.M. Coach Earl Jamison's Office"

COACH EARL JAMISON and PHILIP MAL-LOY in SR acting area. COACH EARL JA-MISON is holding a copy of PHILIP MALLOY's grades. SLIDE: Coach's office, maybe with trophies.

COACH JAMISON: Look, Phil, I've got a copy of your winter term grades here. You know, there's a school rule—a district rule—that you can't be on a team unless you've got a passing grade in every subject.

PHILIP MALLOY: A passing grade?

COACH JAMISON: Yeah. In high school, a passing grade.

PHILIP MALLOY: I didn't know.

COACH JAMISON: Well . . . the point is, Phil, it looks like you don't have high grades. There's a D here. I guess we have a problem.

PHILIP MALLOY: We do?

COACH JAMISON: A D isn't—by the rules—

PHILIP MALLOY: It's Miss Narwin. I keep trying to get her to like me, but she won't.

COACH JAMISON: Is there any point in your talking with her?

PHILIP MALLOY: What do you mean?

COACH JAMISON: The rule...as it stands now, you're not even allowed to try out.

PHILIP MALLOY: I didn't know about that rule.

COACH JAMISON: The rule has been around for a long time. You need passing grades.

PHILIP MALLOY: I mean, you can't kid around with her or anything.

COACH JAMISON: Phil, sometimes you have to go along to get along. That's the whole thing about sports. You have to go with the flow.

PHILIP MALLOY: I think it's a personal thing with her. She has it in for me. I shouldn't be in her class. Could you get me switched?

COACH JAMISON: Maybe if you just talk with her. Do some catch-up work. How about it?

PHILIP MALLOY: I mean, if I knew it was a rule—

COACH JAMISON: Yeah, well, a rule is a rule. It isn't always easy.

PHILIP MALLOY: I didn't know.

SCENE EIGHT

SLIDE: "Tuesday, March 27. 6:23 P.M. The Malloy Kitchen"

BEN and SUSAN MALLOY in UC acting area. SLIDE: Kitchen wall.

SUSAN MALLOY: Honey, did you have a chance to look at Phil's grades?

BEN MALLOY: Uh, sort of. Where is he?

SUSAN MALLOY: In the basement. On your rowing machine. Did you?

BEN MALLOY: I'm looking at them now. Not too bad. Except for English. What's the problem?

SUSAN MALLOY: He says it's the teacher.

BEN MALLOY: I've seen him read.

SUSAN MALLOY: He's reading some paperback. *Insiders. Outsiders.* I don't know. That doesn't seem to be the problem.

BEN MALLOY: I never was one for reading much.

SUSAN MALLOY: Ben, he could flunk that course.

BEN MALLOY: Won't be the end of the world. What would he have to do, go to summer school?

SUSAN MALLOY: The last couple of days he's been very moody.

BEN MALLOY: Come on, he's fourteen.

SUSAN MALLOY: He doesn't want to talk to me. Maybe you should spend more time with him.

BEN MALLOY: I know. But at work I'm all tied up in this—

SUSAN MALLOY: But work's better, isn't it?

BEN MALLOY: Some. (*beat*) Did Phil make the track team?

SUSAN MALLOY: I forgot to ask him. Maybe that's the problem.

BEN MALLOY: I'll talk to him.

SLIDE: "8:05 P.M. The Malloy Basement"

PHILIP MALLOY is in the DC acting area, doing sit-ups. BEN MALLOY enters.

BEN MALLOY: Can I talk to you?

PHILIP MALLOY: Sure.

BEN MALLOY: Uh, Phil . . . school stuff. Straight up. What's the story with English?

PHILIP MALLOY: What do you mean?

BEN MALLOY: I saw your grades. What's with English?

PHILIP MALLOY: You want the truth?

BEN MALLOY: Well?

PHILIP MALLOY: It's the teacher. Narwin. She has it in for me.

BEN MALLOY: How come?

PHILIP MALLOY: I don't know. Nobody likes her.

BEN MALLOY: Want me or your mother to talk to her?

PHILIP MALLOY: No, I can handle it.

BEN MALLOY: What are you reading in school?

PHILIP MALLOY: *Julius Caesar*. Shakespeare.

BEN MALLOY: Uh-oh.

PHILIP MALLOY: *So bad. No one* understands it. Narwin says it's English, but it must have been English before the English got there.

BEN MALLOY: Well, reading is important. (*beat*) How are you getting on with the track team? Phil?

PHILIP MALLOY: I, ah . . . was thinking I wouldn't try out.

BEN MALLOY: But high school track is. . . . Why?

PHILIP MALLOY: Lots of reasons.

BEN MALLOY: Like what? I want to know.

PHILIP MALLOY: Just because you did it doesn't mean I have to.

BEN MALLOY: Now wait a minute. We just got you new shoes. And you're good. Better than I ever was. I love watching you run. And here you are working out. I don't get it. What's going on?

PHILIP MALLOY: Nothing.

BEN MALLOY: Didn't you tell me the coach asked you to be on the team?

PHILIP MALLOY: Doesn't mean. . . . It's my choice.

BEN MALLOY: Phil, let me tell you something. If God gives you a ticket, you better use it.

PHILIP MALLOY: Ticket to what?

BEN MALLOY: Running.

PHILIP MALLOY: I'll think about it.

SLIDE: "9:24 P.M. From a Letter Written by Margaret Narwin to Her Sister"

MARGARET NARWIN in SL acting area. She is holding the letter.

MARGARET NARWIN (*to the audience*): The truth is I'm hurt. Never in all the years I've been at Harrison High have I asked for *anything* in the way of extra funds. If it were a case of *no* money available for *anyone*, I could accept that. But a certain Kimberly Howard, who has been here for only *two* years, and who has a husband who works for some large corporation, *she* receives money! And for some idiotic course in marching band music!

I think there's a question of fairness here. Call it pride, call it vanity, but I would like some respect for all I have done here. From the community. From the administration. (*beat*)

The truth is it's our superintendent's doing. He sent out a memo to everybody warning that the budget vote might fail again. He is a *very* political person. But then, all he wants is to keep his job. I am so angry. . . .

SLIDE: "10:40 P.M. From the Diary of Philip Malloy"

PHILIP MALLOY in the UC acting area. He is holding his diary.

PHILIP MALLOY (*to the audience*): Dad talked to me about the grades. I told him the truth. He seemed to understand. But then he asked me about my being on the track team. I didn't know what to say.

I just realized two things that make me want to puke. Track practice starts tomorrow and I'm *not* on the team. Also, I start homeroom with *Narwin*! I have to find a way to get transferred out.

SCENE NINE

SLIDE: "Wednesday, March 28. 7:30 A.M. Philip and Ken Barchet on the Way to the School Bus"

PHILIP MALLOY and KEN BARCHET in DC acting area.

PHILIP MALLOY: What's happening, man?

KEN BARCHET: Nothing. Got room changes. Who'd you get?

PHILIP MALLOY: Narwin.

KEN BARCHET: So do I. She's okay.

PHILIP MALLOY: Can't stand her.

KEN BARCHET: Doesn't matter. It's just homeroom.

PHILIP MALLOY: No way. I've got her for English, too. I'm going to get transferred out of both.

KEN BARCHET: Why?

PHILIP MALLOY: Told you. I can't stand her.

KEN BARCHET: How you going to do that?

PHILIP MALLOY: I'm working on it.

KEN BARCHET: Sure . . . Malloy Magic, right?

PHILIP MALLOY: You'll see.

SLIDE: "8:03 A.M. Margaret Narwin's Homeroom
        Class"

*MARGARET NARWIN, PHILIP MALLOY,
KEN BARCHET, ALLISON DORESETT, and
LISA GIBBONS in SL acting area. SLIDE:
Classroom wall.*

MARGARET NARWIN: Ladies and gentlemen,
please settle down. For the moment just take any
seat you wish. We'll work out problems later.
Yes?

LISA GIBBONS: Am I supposed to be in this
room?

MARGARET NARWIN: What's your name?

LISA GIBBONS: Lisa Gibbons.

MARGARET NARWIN (*checking her list*): Lisa?
Yes, you're on my list. Just take any seat. Yes,
Allison, you are here.

INTERCOM (*voice of DR GERTRUDE DOANE*): Good morning to all students, faculty, and staff.

MARGARET NARWIN: Please, let's get done with the morning business.

INTERCOM: Today is Wednesday, March twenty-eight. Today will be a Schedule B day. Today in history: In the year A.D. one-ninety-three the Roman Emperor Pertinax was assassinated. On this day in eighteen-sixty-two the Civil War battle in Glorieta, New Mexico, was fought. Please all rise and stand at respectful, silent attention for the playing of our national anthem.

Oh, say, can you see by the dawn's early light . . .

PHILIP MALLOY starts humming.

MARGARET NARWIN: Is that someone humming?

What so proudly we hailed at the twilight's last gleaming?
Whose broad stripes and bright stars . . .

MARGARET NARWIN: Who is that?

. . . thro' the perilous fight,
O'er the ramparts we watched were so gallantly streaming? . . .

MARGARET NARWIN: Is that you, Philip?

PHILIP MALLOY: Just humming.

MARGARET NARWIN: Please stop it.

Gave proof thro' the night that our flag was still there. . . .

PHILIP MALLOY: Mr. Lunser doesn't mind. I just—

MARGARET NARWIN: Stop it now.

PHILIP MALLOY: But—

Oh, say does that star-spangled banner yet wave . . .

MARGARET NARWIN: Now! Thank you.

O'er the land of the free and the home of the brave?

SLIDE: "10:30 A.M. Margaret Narwin and Jacob Benison, Science Teacher, in the Faculty Room"

MARGARET NARWIN and JACOB BENI-SON in DC acting area.

JACOB BENISON: Morning, Peg. How's it going?

MARGARET NARWIN: I'll get through it.

JACOB BENISON: Sometimes I think it's not worth the trouble. I'll be glad to get out of it. Forty-four more days!

MARGARET NARWIN: I sometimes think I should join you.

JACOB BENISON: Can't wait. Get you some coffee? Kim brought in muffins.

MARGARET NARWIN: Kim?

JACOB BENISON: Kimberly Howard. Music.

MARGARET NARWIN: Oh.

JACOB BENISON: Something the matter, Peg?

MARGARET NARWIN: Oh, stupid business. I suppose it's this changing of homeroom classes. The announcements and so on. And when the national anthem comes on, the students are supposed to stand in silence.

JACOB BENISON: Right. I think the rule reads, "Respect, silence, and attention."

MARGARET NARWIN: Exactly. I had a student who started to hum. Very loudly.

JACOB BENISON: Uh-oh. Who was that?

MARGARET NARWIN: Philip Malloy.

JACOB BENISON: Oh, sure. Phil. Nice kid. Bright . . . when he gets around to doing some work. He's got being fast on the brain. Humming? What was he doing that for?

MARGARET NARWIN: I don't know. I had to ask him to stop.

JACOB BENISON: Did he?

MARGARET NARWIN: Not at first. He claimed he always did it in Bernie Lunser's class.

JACOB BENISON: Well, the term won't last forever.

MARGARET NARWIN: Sometimes I wonder.

SLIDE: "12:15 P.M. Philip and Todd Becker in Front of Philip's Locker"

PHILIP MALLOY and TODD BECKER in SL acting area. SLIDE: School hallway.

TODD BECKER: Hey, how come you aren't going out for track?

PHILIP MALLOY: Too much to do.

TODD BECKER: We could use you. Need some power.

PHILIP MALLOY: I'll think about it. Just don't bug me.

TODD BECKER: Just asking. Who's your new homeroom teacher?

PHILIP MALLOY: Narwin.

TODD BECKER: I like her.

PHILIP MALLOY: I hate her.

TODD BECKER: Yeah? How come?

PHILIP MALLOY: You know how they play *The Star-Spangled Banner* in the morning . . . ?

TODD BECKER: Yeah. . . .

PHILIP MALLOY: Well, I started to sing it. . . .

TODD BECKER: Why?

PHILIP MALLOY: Felt like it. She told me to stop.

TODD BECKER: Stop what?

PHILIP MALLOY: Humming.

TODD BECKER: I thought you said singing.

PHILIP MALLOY: Whatever.

TODD BECKER: How come she made you stop?

PHILIP MALLOY: I don't know. She really has it in for me. I mean, she's always on me about something.

TODD BECKER: What did you do?

PHILIP MALLOY: I told you. Nothing.

TODD BECKER: I mean when she told you to stop humming.

PHILIP MALLOY: I stopped. (*beat*) Humming, would you believe it? No way I'm staying in her classes.

SLIDE: "1:40 P.M. Margaret Narwin's English Class"

MARGARET NARWIN, PHILIP MALLOY, and the three STUDENTS in SL acting area. SLIDE: Classroom wall.

MARGARET NARWIN: Now, scene two, line fifty-two. Brutus says, "No, Cassius; for the eye sees not itself / But by reflection, by some other things." What does he mean by that? Anyone? Yes?

STUDENT #1: That he can't see himself.

MARGARET NARWIN: Close. Yes, Philip?

PHILIP MALLOY: But what if he's cross-eyed? He'd see himself then, wouldn't he?

MARGARET NARWIN: I'm not even going to respond to that!

SLIDE: "3:15 P.M. Philip and Allison on the School Bus"

PHILIP MALLOY and ALLISON DORESETT in DC acting area.

ALLISON DORESETT: Can I sit next to you?

PHILIP MALLOY: Oh, sure.

ALLISON DORESETT: What's the matter? You look like death warmed over.

PHILIP MALLOY: I'm okay.

ALLISON DORESETT: You got Miss Narwin mad today with that joke.

PHILIP MALLOY: She's always mad at me.

ALLISON DORESETT: Is something the matter?

PHILIP MALLOY: Nothing.

ALLISON DORESETT: How come you didn't go to track tryouts?

PHILIP MALLOY (*shrugs*): Had to do something.

ALLISON DORESETT: Todd said you were really great.

PHILIP MALLOY: Yeah.

ALLISON DORESETT: Boy, you're in a mood!

PHILIP MALLOY: Just don't feel like talking.

ALLISON DORESETT: Well, excuse me!

ALLISON DORESETT exits.

PHILIP MALLOY: Hey, Allison, wait. . . . Damn!

SLIDE: "3:20 P.M. Margaret Narwin and Bernard Lunser Outside the School's Main Office"

MARGARET NARWIN and BERNARD LUNSER in SR acting area. SLIDE: School hallway.

MARGARET NARWIN: Bernie! I need to ask you something.

BERNARD LUNSER: What's that?

MARGARET NARWIN: Do you allow your students to sing the national anthem in your morning homeroom?

BERNARD LUNSER: Sing? I thought the kids are supposed to be quiet.

MARGARET NARWIN: One of my new homeroom students informed me that you always allow singing. Do you?

BERNARD LUNSER: The rule says keep quiet. . . .

MARGARET NARWIN: But do you allow singing?

BERNARD LUNSER: Hey, Peg, do I look like a guy who goes around breaking important rules?

MARGARET NARWIN: Thanks.

SLIDE: "7:15 P.M. Discussion between Philip and His Parents During Dinner"

PHILIP MALLOY plus BEN and SUSAN MALLOY at the dinner table in the UC acting area. They are eating dinner, which can be mimed. SLIDE: Kitchen wall.

BEN MALLOY: What did you decide to do about the track team? (*pause*)

SUSAN MALLOY: Philip, your father asked you something.

PHILIP MALLOY: I'm not on the team.

BEN MALLOY: I know that. But I'd like to know why.

PHILIP MALLOY: What would you say if a teacher said I wasn't allowed to sing *The Star-Spangled Banner*?

38

BEN MALLOY: Anywhere?

PHILIP MALLOY: In class.

SUSAN MALLOY: What's this have to do with your running?

PHILIP MALLOY: I'm trying to tell you. You know, when school starts, homeroom, when they play the song over the speaker system. It's a tape.

BEN MALLOY: Come again?

PHILIP MALLOY: I'm trying to explain!

BEN MALLOY: No need to raise your voice!

SUSAN MALLOY: The both of you. . . .

BEN MALLOY: Philip, just tell us what. . . . Obviously, something has happened. Why are you upset?

PHILIP MALLOY: Everybody got new homeroom teachers in school today. Anyway, I got this Miss Narwin. She's a real bitch.

BEN MALLOY: Phil!

PHILIP MALLOY: Do you want to know what happened or not?

SUSAN MALLOY: Honey, let the boy tell it his way.

PHILIP MALLOY: So they always start off play-ing *The Star-Spangled Banner*. Okay. It's stupid, but, sometimes I sort of sing along. . . . Or I hum. No big deal. But this teacher got real mad and yelled at me.

BEN MALLOY: She yelled at you because you were—?

PHILIP MALLOY: Right. Humming. That's all I was doing.

BEN MALLOY: And she yelled at you?

SUSAN MALLOY: That's not what I'd call fair.

PHILIP MALLOY: Yeah.

SLIDE: "8:32 P.M. From a Letter Written by Mar-garet Narwin to Her Sister"

MARGARET NARWIN in DC acting area. She is holding the letter.

MARGARET NARWIN (*to the audience*): I do think it's the best thing Barbara Pym ever wrote. It was so soothing to come home to that quiet, thoughtful, civilized British world. (*beat*) The truth is, I needed something soothing. Today was "Spring Changeover Day," when our stu-dents, after six months of struggling to learn ex-actly where to go, are tossed pell-mell here, there, anywhere. Of course, bedlam is *always* the result. But one has to be vigilant and *firm*. As well as consistent and fair. That's the key with students these days. Sometimes I haven't the stamina for it. Ah, well. . . .

SLIDE: "9:05 P.M. From the Diary of Philip Malloy"

PHILIP MALLOY in UC acting area. He is holding his diary.

PHILIP MALLOY (*to the audience*): Today was rotten. Nothing was right. I felt like punching Narwin in the face. It all just stinks.

SLIDE: "10:45 P.M. Philip and His Father in His Bedroom"

PHILIP MALLOY and BEN MALLOY in UC acting area. SLIDE: PHILIP MALLOY's bedroom.

BEN MALLOY: Now, look, about this business about not being allowed to sing the national anthem—

PHILIP MALLOY: I was humming.

BEN MALLOY: Whatever. Now, your mother and I want you to understand that whatever it is, we're on your side.

PHILIP MALLOY: I didn't think you were interested.

BEN MALLOY: Of course I'm interested.

PHILIP MALLOY: It's just that the teacher—

BEN MALLOY: No, wait. Straight up, I think she's wrong. You're right to be bugged. Now, your mother and I are no great—well—big patriots. But that doesn't mean we don't love our country. We just don't make a big thing about it. But not being allowed to sing *The Star-Spangled Banner* . . . well, that's sort of like not being allowed to pray. A personal thing. The point is, in America, it doesn't seem right. And we just want you to know we're with you.

PHILIP MALLOY: Thanks. (*beat*) You're not mad?

BEN MALLOY: Of course not. I have half a mind to talk to Ted Griffen. He's running for school board. That can mean something.

PHILIP MALLOY: He's always chasing me off his lawn.

BEN MALLOY: Yeah. But you were a kid then. Phil, let me tell you something. You really have to stick up for your rights. Your mother and I will stand with you. Don't worry.

PHILIP MALLOY: Right.

SCENE TEN

SLIDE: "Thursday, March 29. 8:02 A.M. Margaret
　　　　Narwin's Homeroom Class"

MARGARET NARWIN, PHILIP MALLOY,
STUDENT #1, and STUDENT #3 in SL acting
area. SLIDE: Classroom wall.

MARGARET NARWIN: Ladies and gentlemen,
please take your assigned seats. I need to take attendance.

STUDENT #3: Miss Narwin.

MARGARET NARWIN: Yes?

STUDENT #3: Peggy Lord is sick.

MARGARET NARWIN: Thank you.

INTERCOM (*voice of DR. GERTRUDE DOANE*):
Good morning to all students, faculty, and staff.
Today is Thursday, March twenty-nine. Today
will be a Schedule A day. Today in history: In
the year seventeen-ninety our tenth president,
John Tyler, was born. In nineteen-eighteen singer
Pearl Bailey was born. Please rise and stand at

respectful, silent attention for the playing of our national anthem.

Oh, say, can you see by the dawn's early light . . .

PHILIP MALLOY starts humming.

MARGARET NARWIN: Philip, is that you again?

What so proudly we hailed at the twilight's last gleaming?
Whose broad stripes and bright stars . . .

MARGARET NARWIN: I spoke with you yesterday about this.

. . . thro' the perilous fight,
O'er the ramparts we watched were so gallantly streaming?

MARGARET NARWIN: Now, please, stop it.

And the rockets' red glare, the bombs bursting in air . . .
Gave proof thro' the night that our flag was still there . . .

MARGARET NARWIN: Philip, leave this room instantly. Report to Dr. Palleni's office. Now!

SLIDE: "8:35 A.M. Dr. Joseph Palleni's Office"

PHILIP MALLOY and DR. JOSEPH PALLENI in SR acting area. SLIDE: Office wall.

DR. PALLENI: You must have some idea about what seems to be the problem. Miss Narwin asked you to leave the class. What happened?

PHILIP MALLOY: She wouldn't let me sing *The Star-Spangled Banner*.

DR. PALLENI: What?

PHILIP MALLOY: It's just a thing I like to do. Sing along.

DR. PALLENI: You mean, when the morning tape plays? . . .

PHILIP MALLOY: Yeah.

DR. PALLENI: There's a rule about being quiet at that time.

PHILIP MALLOY: Yeah, well, it's sort of a . . . patriotic thing with me. But the whole thing is, she always has it in for me.

DR. PALLENI: Did Miss Narwin ask you to stop?

PHILIP MALLOY: I wasn't being loud or anything like that.

DR. PALLENI: But when Miss Narwin asked you, did you stop?

PHILIP MALLOY: It was just to myself.

DR. PALLENI (*looking through a desk drawer*): Where is that thing? Here it is. This is a memo from Dr. Doane. Go on, read it. What does it say? "Silent." Right? But you were singing. Miss Narwin asked you to stop singing. You didn't. You were disobedient. So she asked you to leave.

PHILIP MALLOY: How can you ask someone not to sing *The Star-Spangled Banner*?

DR. PALLENI: It's the rule.

PHILIP MALLOY: Is a memo a rule?

DR. PALLENI: Philip, look, I've got more important things to do with my time than argue with you about following simple, basic rules.

PHILIP MALLOY: Put me in another homeroom. And another English class.

DR. PALLENI: What's English have to do with this? (*pause*) Philip, I asked you something.

PHILIP MALLOY: She and I don't get along.

DR. PALLENI: Look, Philip, you are here to get an education. You've given me your side of the story. I'll check with Miss Narwin, but it seems pretty clear to me. . . . Here's a note that says I spoke to you. Scoot.

PHILIP MALLOY: But—

DR. PALLENI: Hey, Phil, be cool. I heard you're a runner. It's a great day for running. Go join the track team. They could use you. Have a nice day.

SLIDE: "6:10 P.M. The Malloy Kitchen"

BEN and SUSAN MALLOY in UC acting area.
SLIDE: Kitchen wall.

SUSAN MALLOY: What's wrong?

BEN MALLOY: I got chewed out by Dexter.

SUSAN MALLOY: What for?

BEN MALLOY: Some job estimate that went wrong. Wasn't even anything I did.

SUSAN MALLOY: I hope you stood up for yourself.

BEN MALLOY: And get myself in his bad books?

SUSAN MALLOY: You wouldn't get yourself—

BEN MALLOY: You don't understand. I'm sorry I mentioned it. Look, I'm just not in a position of power there. Okay? Just forget it.

SUSAN MALLOY: Sorry I asked.

SLIDE: "7:10 P.M. The Malloy Kitchen"

PHILIP MALLOY plus BEN and SUSAN MALLOY. SLIDE: Kitchen wall.

PHILIP MALLOY: It happened again.

SUSAN MALLOY: What happened?

PHILIP MALLOY: In school. This morning I was singing *The Star-Spangled Banner*. The teacher kicked me out. She sent me to the assistant principal's office.

BEN MALLOY: I hope you stood up for yourself.

SUSAN MALLOY: What did he say?

PHILIP MALLOY: He sided with Narwin.

BEN MALLOY: Listen to me. Don't give in to that crap. There must be some mistake.

PHILIP MALLOY: That's the way she is.

BEN MALLOY: You have to stick up for yourself, Phil. We'll stand behind you.

SLIDE: "9:45 P.M. From a Letter Written by Margaret Narwin to Her Sister"

MARGARET NARWIN in DC acting area. She is holding the letter.

MARGARET NARWIN (*to the audience*): So you see, Anita, it was gratifying to hear Gertrude talk this way . . . exactly the kind of support teachers need. Certainly it's what I needed. Many teachers have almost nothing good to say about their administrators, complaining that they fail to support them. Or that they show only slight concern about their problems. My principal is different. I'm lucky. . . .

SLIDE: "11:05 P.M. From the Diary of Philip Malloy"

PHILIP MALLOY in UC acting area. He is holding his diary.

PHILIP MALLOY (*to the audience*): Lots of kids bad-mouth their parents, say they never stick up for them or understand them or pay any attention to them. Stuff like that. My parents are different. I'm lucky.

SCENE ELEVEN

SLIDE: "Friday, March 30. 8:05 A.M. Margaret Nar-
    win's Homeroom Class"

*MARGARET NARWIN, PHILIP MALLOY,
STUDENT #1, and STUDENT #2 in SL acting
area. SLIDE (which remains on through the end
of the scene): Classroom wall.*

*PHILIP MALLOY is singing along with the
tape, which is being broadcast over the intercom
system.*

**What so proudly we hailed at the twilight's last gleam-
ing?**
**Whose broad stripes and bright stars, thro' the perilous
fight . . .**

MARGARET NARWIN: Philip, is that you singing again?

PHILIP MALLOY: I have the right to do it.

**O'er the ramparts we watched were so gallantly stream-
ing?**
And the rockets' red glare, the bombs bursting in air . . .

50

MARGARET NARWIN: The what?

PHILIP MALLOY: The right.

Gave proof thro' the night that our flag was still there. . . .

MARGARET NARWIN: I want you to stop it immediately. Your actions are thoroughly disrespectful.

PHILIP MALLOY: It's you who's being disrespectful.

Oh, say does that star-spangled banner yet wave . . .

MARGARET NARWIN: Philip!

PHILIP MALLOY: I'm being patriotic. It's a free country. You have no right to stop me.

MARGARET NARWIN: Philip Malloy, you will leave this room immediately! Report to the principal's office.

PHILIP MALLOY: You can't keep me from being patriotic.

MARGARET NARWIN: Leave!

PHILIP MALLOY crosses to SR acting area, which has now become Dr. Palleni's office. DR. JOSEPH PALLENI enters and sits behind the desk. SLIDE (which remains on through the end of the scene): Office wall.

DR. PALLENI: Something happened. What's going on?

PHILIP MALLOY: Miss Narwin, she won't let me sing *The Star-Spangled Banner*.

DR. PALLENI: Isn't this what we were talking about the last time?

PHILIP MALLOY: She's against me being patriotic.

DR. PALLENI: I thought we agreed that when we have rules in schools, we stick with them.

PHILIP MALLOY: Get me out of her classes.

DR. PALLENI: Look, Philip, what do you want me to do? Change the rules just for you?

PHILIP MALLOY: No, but . . . she's wrong. I was just singing. That's all.

DR. PALLENI: That's all you have to say?

PHILIP MALLOY: It's a free country.

DR. PALLENI: Nothing is free.

PHILIP MALLOY: Get me out of her classes.

DR. PALLENI: Phil, sit out in the hall for a while. Cool off. Otherwise, I call your folks, they come get you—boom!—two-day suspension. Automatic.

PHILIP MALLOY: But she's wrong.

DR. PALLENI: I'll level with you, Philip. You're the one who is wrong. You're here to get an education. Rules are rules. Now clear out.

DR. JOSEPH PALLENI crosses to SL acting area.

DR. PALLENI: Excuse me, Miss Narwin, may I have a word with you?

MARGARET NARWIN: Class, continue on with that scene. I'll be right back.

DR. PALLENI: Sorry to bother you, Peg, but it's about Phil Malloy.

MARGARET NARWIN: Something is certainly bothering that boy.

DR. PALLENI: Any idea what it's about?

MARGARET NARWIN: No.

DR. PALLENI: I offered to get him out of this business by giving him the chance to come back and apologize, but he won't.

MARGARET NARWIN: Maybe it would be better to switch him into another homeroom.

DR. PALLENI: That's what he suggested. And out of your English class, too.

MARGARET NARWIN: He's doing poorly there.

DR. PALLENI: Let's start with a homeroom change. The parents might want to talk with you.

MARGARET NARWIN: I understand. I wish I could reach him.

DR. PALLENI: Yeah, a good kid. Maybe something going on at home. Or hormones. Does he have a girlfriend?

MARGARET NARWIN: Joe, I wouldn't know.

MARGARET NARWIN returns to her class.

DR. JOSEPH PALLENI crosses back to SR acting area.

DR. PALLENI: Now, Philip, Miss Narwin is in agreement with you. You did break the rules. She also said that she is prepared to let bygones be bygones if you apologize and promise not to do it again.

PHILIP MALLOY: No.

DR. PALLENI: It would be a shame to put something down on your record. But I'm prepared to call one of your parents to come get you. You'll be out for the rest of the day and. . . . How about Monday? Give you a long weekend to think it over.

PHILIP MALLOY: I'm not going to change my mind.

DR. PALLENI: Okay, who do you want me to call?

PHILIP MALLOY: My father doesn't like to be called at work.

DR. PALLENI: Too bad. Is your mother reachable? (*pause*) Phil?

PHILIP MALLOY: She works too.

DR. PALLENI: Where?

PHILIP MALLOY: At the telephone company.

DR. PALLENI: I'll call her. (*beat*) Last chance, Phil.

PHILIP MALLOY: Can't you just—

DR. PALLENI: An apology.

PHILIP MALLOY: Call her.

DR. JOSEPH PALLENI picks up the phone.

SUSAN MALLOY in DC acting area.

DR. PALLENI: Hello? Is this Mrs. Malloy, Phil's mother?

SUSAN MALLOY: Yes, it is.

DR. PALLENI: This is Dr. Palleni, assistant principal at Harrison High. I'm afraid we've had a little incident here . . . rule-breaking.

SUSAN MALLOY: What happened?

DR. PALLENI: And breaking the rule twice in one week after he'd been warned.

SUSAN MALLOY: What rule?

DR. PALLENI: Philip was offered a chance to apologize to the teacher, but he won't. So, I'm afraid—and let me stress that this is Phil's decision, not mine—what we have here is a two-day suspension. I'm afraid you'll have to come and take him home.

SUSAN MALLOY: Now?

DR. PALLENI: Yes.

SUSAN MALLOY: What rule did he break?

DR. PALLENI: We—you, me, and Philip—can talk about it when you get here.

SUSAN MALLOY: I'll get permission and then come right over.

DR. PALLENI: Thank you.

SLIDE: "10:05 A.M. Phone Conversation between Philip Malloy's Parents"

SUSAN MALLOY in DC acting area. BEN MALLOY in UC acting area.

BEN MALLOY: What's up?

SUSAN MALLOY: I have to go and get Phil at the school. They're going to suspend him.

BEN MALLOY: Why?

SUSAN MALLOY: Some rule. I'm really upset.

BEN MALLOY: I'm going to give them a piece of my mind.

SUSAN MALLOY: Don't you think we should—

BEN MALLOY: Susan, the kid has done nothing!

SUSAN MALLOY: We can speak—

BEN MALLOY: Honey, I have to go. Something just came up.

SLIDE: "10:42 A.M. Dr. Palleni's Office"

DR. JOSEPH PALLENI, PHILIP MALLOY, and SUSAN MALLOY in SR acting area. SLIDE: Office wall.

DR. PALLENI: Philip broke a rule. Twice. He and I talked it over earlier this week and I made it clear what would happen. If a student creates a disturbance in a classroom, that's breaking the rule. An important rule. Now, we offered Philip an opportunity to apologize. I'll offer it again. Philip?

PHILIP MALLOY: She really dislikes me.

DR. PALLENI: Who is that?

PHILIP MALLOY: Narwin.

SUSAN MALLOY: Philip has been saying that—

DR. PALLENI: Look, Mrs. Malloy, Philip admits that he broke a rule.

SUSAN MALLOY: What rule?

DR. PALLENI: Disturbing a class.

PHILIP MALLOY: Singing the national anthem.

SUSAN MALLOY: Is that the rule?

DR. PALLENI: Yes, disturbing the class.

SUSAN MALLOY: I just can't believe that—

DR. PALLENI: Excuse me. Philip, did you break the rule?

PHILIP MALLOY: It's a dumb rule.

DR. PALLENI: See? Mrs. Malloy, it is my job to make sure the school works together in harmony—the kids, the staff, and the teachers. We can't have the students deciding which rules to follow and which rules not to follow. I'll have to suspend Philip for the rest of today. And Monday. Be back on Tuesday.

SUSAN MALLOY: I just want to say that I don't think this is right.

DR. PALLENI: Excuse me. Are you saying that kids should only follow the rules they want to?

SUSAN MALLOY: No, but—

DR. PALLENI: Then we're in agreement. Thank you for coming in.

SLIDE: "11:02 A.M. Conversation between Philip and His Mother on Their Way Home"

PHILIP MALLOY and SUSAN MALLOY in the DC acting area.

SUSAN MALLOY: Phil, what *is* this all about?

PHILIP MALLOY: I told you, Narwin . . .

SUSAN MALLOY: You've never been suspended.

PHILIP MALLOY: It's her.

SUSAN MALLOY: But why?

PHILIP MALLOY: I don't know.

SUSAN MALLOY: They said you could apologize.

PHILIP MALLOY: There's nothing to apologize for.

SUSAN MALLOY: We'll talk it out with your father when he gets home tonight.

PHILIP MALLOY: Yeah, well, he told me I should stick up for myself. That she was wrong and I was right.

SUSAN MALLOY: Sometimes I think we should have sent you to Washington Academy.

PHILIP MALLOY: Geeky private school? No way.

MARGARET NARWIN and DR. JOSEPH PALLENI in DC acting area.

DR. PALLENI: Oh, Peg! I know you're rushing off. Look, I just want you to know I took care of the Malloy boy. Talked to his mother. She understands. Couple of days' suspension. No big deal.

MARGARET NARWIN: Did you have to suspend him?

DR. PALLENI: Two infractions in one week. I put a memo in your box. Also, switched him back to Bernie Lunser for homeroom. What about his English class?

MARGARET NARWIN: I don't want to give up on him yet.

DR. PALLENI: Whatever you say.

MARGARET NARWIN: He's really a nice boy. Thanks for taking care of it.

DR. PALLENI: No problem.

SLIDE: "3:45 P.M. Phone Conversation between Ken and Allison"

*KEN BARCHET and ALLISON DORESETT
at opposite sides of SL acting area.*

ALLISON DORESETT: Is this Ken?

KEN BARCHET: Yeah.

ALLISON DORESETT: This is Allison Doresett.

KEN BARCHET: Oh, hi.

ALLISON DORESETT: Is it true that Phil got suspended?

KEN BARCHET: Yeah.

ALLISON DORESETT: Why?

KEN BARCHET: You were there.

ALLISON DORESETT: The singing?

KEN BARCHET: Yeah. Narwin got him kicked out.

ALLISON DORESETT: You're kidding. She wouldn't do that.

KEN BARCHET: She did. You saw it.

ALLISON DORESETT: For how long?

KEN BARCHET: Two days.

ALLISON DORSETT: Wow. He must have really gotten on her nerves. Well, I just wanted to know. People are talking.

KEN BARCHET: What are they saying?

ALLISON DORSETT: You know. Weird.

SLIDE: "6:45 P.M. Discussion between Philip Malloy's Parents"

BEN and SUSAN MALLOY in UC acting area. SLIDE: Kitchen wall.

BEN MALLOY: Where's Philip?

SUSAN MALLOY: Up in the shower. He just got back from running.

BEN MALLOY: You talk with him about what happened?

SUSAN MALLOY: When I drove him home. But I had to get right back to work. It's just what I told you. How was your day?

BEN MALLOY: Rotten. Dexter is still sore at me.

SLIDE: "7:00 P.M. From a Letter Written by Margaret Narwin to Her Sister"

MARGARET NARWIN in DC acting area. She is holding the letter.

MARGARET NARWIN (*to the audience*): Do you remember my writing to you about Philip Malloy? I'm convinced there is something going on in this boy's private life that is deeply troubling him. Twice this week I had to send him out for being disruptive. Our society is always asking schools to do what is not done at home. Then Joe Palleni, the assistant principal, felt compelled to suspend him for a bit—something I *never* believe is productive. Philip is a nice boy, so I do feel badly about the whole thing. Next week, when he comes back, I intend to sit down with him and have a heart-to-heart talk.

SLIDE: "7:12 P.M. The Malloy Kitchen"

PHILIP MALLOY plus BEN and SUSAN MALLOY in UC acting area. SLIDE: Kitchen wall.

BEN MALLOY: We're on your side. But I have to know what happened.

PHILIP MALLOY: See, they play *The Star-Spangled Banner* at the beginning of school.... A tape.

BEN MALLOY: Okay.

PHILIP MALLOY: When I was in Mr. Lunser's class, he was like, almost asking me to sing out loud. But this teacher—

BEN MALLOY: Mrs. Narwin.

PHILIP MALLOY: It's Miss.

BEN MALLOY: Figures.

SUSAN MALLOY: That has nothing to do with it, Ben!

BEN MALLOY: Go on.

PHILIP MALLOY: She won't let me. She threw me out of class.

SUSAN MALLOY: The principal said it was the rule.

PHILIP MALLOY: The *assistant* principal.

BEN MALLOY: But why does that mean suspension?

PHILIP MALLOY: She threw me out twice this week.

BEN MALLOY: It seems arbitrary.

SUSAN MALLOY: Stupid rules.

BEN MALLOY: Right. How can you have a rule against singing *The Star-Spangled Banner*?

PHILIP MALLOY: Ask Narwin.

BEN MALLOY: You know who I bet would be interested in this?

PHILIP MALLOY: Who?

BEN MALLOY: Ted Griffen.

SUSAN MALLOY: Why?

BEN MALLOY: He's a neighbor. A friend. And he's running for school board. He should be interested. That's what the board does. Keeps the schools in line.

PHILIP MALLOY: He won't be able to do anything. If I could just get out of her classes . . .

BEN MALLOY: Maybe. Maybe not. But Phil, we intend to support you on this.

SLIDE: "8:40 P.M. Conversation between Philip Malloy, Ben Malloy, and Ted Griffen"

PHILIP MALLOY, BEN MALLOY, and TED GRIFFEN in DC acting area. TED GRIFFEN holding a telephone.

BEN MALLOY: Got a minute, Ted? This a bad time?

TED GRIFFEN: Well, I am in the middle of a talk with . . . why, what's up?

BEN MALLOY: Something about school. And Phil here . . .

TED GRIFFEN: I'm not on the school board yet, Ben. Trying, but not yet.

BEN MALLOY: That's the point. Phil was suspended for singing *The Star-Spangled Banner*.

TED GRIFFEN: What?

BEN MALLOY: He was kicked out of school for singing the national anthem.

TED GRIFFEN: Are you serious?

BEN MALLOY: I know. It's crazy.

TED GRIFFEN (*to PHILIP MALLOY*): That true?

PHILIP MALLOY: Yes, sir.

BEN MALLOY: We couldn't believe it at first either. But they called Susan at work to bring him home. Two-day suspension. For *singing*.

TED GRIFFEN: Who did it?

BEN MALLOY: The principal.

PHILIP MALLOY: Assistant principal.

TED GRIFFEN: Were you singing?

BEN MALLOY: Tell him.

PHILIP MALLOY: They play the national anthem in the morning. And I . . . I was singing it. Mostly to myself. Then, I have this teacher . . . and she threw me out of the class and—

TED GRIFFEN: Wait a minute. I want to get this straight. Look, I have a reporter I'm talking to. Jennifer Stewart, from the *Manchester Record*. School beat. How about talking to me with her there?

BEN MALLOY (*to PHILIP MALLOY*): What do you say?

PHILIP MALLOY: A reporter?

TED GRIFFEN: She's covering the school board elections around the state. A good person.

PHILIP MALLOY: I don't know. . . .

TED GRIFFEN: Very straightforward. I'd like her to hear about this. Just tell her the truth. You don't mind, do you, Ben?

BEN MALLOY: No.

TED GRIFFEN: Phil?

PHILIP MALLOY: Well . . .

TED GRIFFEN: Sure. Just tell her the truth. Nothing but the truth. Come on.

*PHILIP MALLOY in UC acting area. He is
holding his diary.*

PHILIP MALLOY (*to the audience*): It really hit
the fan today. So much happened I have a head-
ache. It's going to take a while to think out. Actually, I don't feel so great. In a way, the whole
thing is stupid. But everybody says I was right.
(*beat*) And I was.

SCENE TWELVE

SLIDE: "Saturday, March 31. 10:00 A.M. Phone conversation between Jennifer Stewart of the *Manchester Record* and Dr. Albert Seymour, Superintendent of Schools"

JENNIFER STEWART and DR. ALBERT SEYMOUR on opposite sides of the DC acting area.

JENNIFER STEWART: May I speak to Dr. Albert Seymour, please.

DR. SEYMOUR: Speaking.

JENNIFER STEWART: Dr. Seymour, this is Jennifer Stewart of the *Manchester Record*. I'm the education reporter. I hope you don't mind a call at home.

DR. SEYMOUR: Oh, no.

JENNIFER STEWART: I wanted to check some facts with you.

DR. SEYMOUR: Certainly.

JENNIFER STEWART: Sir, does the Harrison School District have a rule that forbids students from singing *The Star-Spangled Banner*?

DR. SEYMOUR: Of course not. Whatever gave you that idea?

JENNIFER STEWART: There's been a claim.

DR. SEYMOUR: Hogwash. You should check your sources.

JENNIFER STEWART: I'm checking them right now.

DR. SEYMOUR: The answer is no. We do not have such a rule. Absolutely.

JENNIFER STEWART: May I quote you?

DR. SEYMOUR: Of course.

JENNIFER STEWART: Thank you.

SLIDE: "10:15 A.M. Phone Conversation between Jennifer Stewart and Dr. Gertrude Doane, Principal, Harrison High"

JENNIFER STEWART and DR. GERTRUDE DOANE in DC acting area, except JENNIFER STEWART is on the opposite side of the area from where she was in the previous scene.

JENNIFER STEWART: May I speak to Dr. Doane, please.

DR. DOANE: This is she.

JENNIFER STEWART: Dr. Doane, this is Jennifer Stewart, of the *Manchester Record*. I do the school stories. Sorry to bother you on a Saturday.

DR. DOANE: Yes?

JENNIFER STEWART: I'm checking out an item that's come to our attention. It would appear that one of your students, Philip Malloy—

DR. DOANE: Ninth grade.

JENNIFER STEWART: You know him?

DR. DOANE: Oh, yes. Nice boy. Know him well. Has something happened to him?

JENNIFER STEWART: This is in reference to his suspension from school.

DR. DOANE: Suspension?

JENNIFER STEWART: Isn't that something that as principal you would know about?

DR. DOANE: Oh, yes. . . .

JENNIFER STEWART: Philip Malloy claims, as his parents claim, that he was suspended yesterday for two days.

DR. DOANE: Discipline problems are usually in the hands of my assistant principal, Dr. Palleni.

JENNIFER STEWART: Wouldn't Dr. Palleni discuss such a suspension with you first?

DR. DOANE: That would depend on . . . Ms. . . . .

JENNIFER STEWART: Stewart.

DR. DOANE: Ms. Stewart, I'm not sure I should be discussing this matter with you. Records regarding our children are of a confidential nature.

JENNIFER STEWART: It's already a matter of public record. The boy and his father made a public statement. They claim he was suspended.

DR. DOANE: That's what you say. You call me up and inform me about something of which I have had no prior information.

JENNIFER STEWART: Then you didn't know about this? Ms. Doane—

DR. DOANE: *Dr*. Doane.

JENNIFER STEWART: Excuse me, Dr. Doane, Philip Malloy, who is a student at your school, and who you claim to know well, has made a

73

statement to the effect that he was suspended for singing *The Star-Spangled Banner*.

DR. DOANE: Oh, really!

JENNIFER STEWART: His father claims this is true. I just spoke to your superintendent . . .

DR. DOANE: Dr. Seymour?

JENNIFER STEWART: That's right. And he says that Harrison School District has no such rule. I'm just trying . . .

DR. DOANE: I see no reason to be talking to a reporter about a student's problem. In any case, it doesn't seem to have happened. The superintendent told you we have no such rule.

JENNIFER STEWART: Would a student in your school run into difficulty by singing the national anthem?

DR. DOANE: Of course not. But I repeat: Discipline problems of a minor nature are handled by my assistant principal.

JENNIFER STEWART: Palleni?

DR. DOANE: That's right. Dr. Joseph Palleni.

JENNIFER STEWART: Thank you.

PHILIP MALLOY and SUSAN MALLOY in UC acting area. PHILIP MALLOY has a letter in his hand. SLIDE: Kitchen wall.

PHILIP MALLOY: Hey, Ma, look at this letter! It just came in the mail. They shifted me out of Narwin's homeroom class. Back to Mr. Lunser.

SUSAN MALLOY: Well, that's something. They must have seen that something was wrong. Maybe you can go back to school Monday.

PHILIP MALLOY: Says it won't happen till Tuesday. When I go back.

SUSAN MALLOY: May be just as well. I won't want you to have to deal with that woman again.

PHILIP MALLOY: But I still have her for English.

SUSAN MALLOY: Didn't they change that?

PHILIP MALLOY: No.

SUSAN MALLOY: But if they admit they're wrong about the one thing . . .

PHILIP MALLOY: Bet they forgot to say that. Where's Dad?

SUSAN MALLOY: He went to the store. Feel better?

PHILIP MALLOY: Yeah. But the English . . .

SUSAN MALLOY: You just said they forgot.

PHILIP MALLOY: I guess.

SLIDE: "10:40 A.M. Conversation between Jennifer Stewart and Dr. Joseph Palleni, Assistant Principal, Harrison High"

JENNIFER STEWART and DR. JOSEPH PALLENI in DC acting area, except JENNIFER STEWART is on the opposite side of the area from where she was in the previous scene.

DR. PALLENI: Hello. This is Dr. Palleni.

JENNIFER STEWART: Dr. Palleni, this is Jennifer Stewart. I'm a reporter for the *Manchester Record*. I've already spoken with your—

DR. PALLENI: What is this about?

JENNIFER STEWART: Dr. Palleni, according to Dr. Seymour, the Harrison School District has no rule that would keep a student from singing *The Star-Spangled Banner*.

DR. PALLENI: Did you say *singing*?

JENNIFER STEWART: Yes. Is that your under-
standing?

DR. PALLENI: Well . . .

JENNIFER STEWART: Now Dr. Doane, your
principal, says that you are in charge of discipline in the school.

DR. PALLENI: *With* her. I always keep her informed.

JENNIFER STEWART: Did you inform her that
on Friday you suspended a student, Philip Malloy, for singing *The Star-Spangled Banner*?

DR. PALLENI: I did no such thing!

JENNIFER STEWART: You didn't inform her or
you didn't suspend the boy? Which? (*pause*) Dr.
Palleni? Are you still there?

DR. PALLENI: I don't wish to talk to you.

JENNIFER STEWART: No comment?

DR. PALLENI: No comment. But you've got
your facts all wrong.

JENNIFER STEWART: Is that your comment?

DR. PALLENI: No comment.

JENNIFER STEWART: I'm sorry. Should I call you back?

DR. PALLENI: Not to talk about this.

JENNIFER STEWART: May I quote you?

SLIDE: "11:00 A.M. Phone Conversation between Jennifer Stewart and Margaret Narwin"

JENNIFER STEWART and MARGARET NARWIN in DC acting area, except JENNIFER STEWART is on the opposite side of the area from where she was in the previous scene.

JENNIFER STEWART: Margaret Narwin, please.

MARGARET NARWIN: Speaking.

JENNIFER STEWART: Miss Narwin, my name is Jennifer Stewart, of the *Manchester Record*. The education reporter. I'm trying to write a story regarding an incident . . . something that appears to have happened in one of your classes. I understand you are a teacher.

MARGARET NARWIN: An English teacher. Yes.

JENNIFER STEWART: Have you taught there long?

MARGARET NARWIN: For twenty-one years. What incident are you referring to? I'm not aware . . .

78

JENNIFER STEWART: I'm simply trying to get the facts correct. I'm sure you can appreciate that.

MARGARET NARWIN: Are you sure this has something to do with me?

JENNIFER STEWART: That appears to be the case. I spoke to your superintendent, your principal, and your assistant principal, as well as Philip Malloy and his father.

MARGARET NARWIN: Who?

JENNIFER STEWART: Philip Malloy. I believe he is one of your students.

MARGARET NARWIN: Well . . .

JENNIFER STEWART: Now, as I understand it, the boy was suspended from school because he sang *The Star-Spangled Banner* in your class. He says it's a question of patriotism with him. (*pause*) Miss Narwin? Are you there?

MARGARET NARWIN: Yes. . . .

JENNIFER STEWART: Could you give me your side of the story?

MARGARET NARWIN: The boy was creating a disturbance.

JENNIFER STEWART: By singing the national anthem?

MARGARET NARWIN: We have a rule . . .

JENNIFER STEWART: Your superintendent, Dr. Seymour, says there is no rule.

MARGARET NARWIN: I don't think I should be talking about this.

JENNIFER STEWART: But you do acknowledge that you sent him from your room?

MARGARET NARWIN: I think you need to speak to our principal.

JENNIFER STEWART: I did speak with her.

MARGARET NARWIN: Then I have nothing more to say.

JENNIFER STEWART: Are you sure?

MARGARET NARWIN: Quite sure.

JENNIFER STEWART: Thank you, Miss . . . or is it *Mrs*. Narwin?

MARGARET NARWIN: Miss.

JENNIFER STEWART: Thank you.

PHILIP MALLOY in a spotlight in UC acting area. He is holding his diary.

PHILIP MALLOY (*to the audience*): Aside from getting out of Narwin's homeroom, not much of anything today. Boring! Newspapers to deliver. Collection day. Can't understand how people who want the paper think they can get away with not paying for it. And it comes out of my pocket. Then folks made me do yard work. Clean up room. Ken came over. Been trying to figure a way to get on the school track team. Maybe— like the coach said—I should ask Narwin for extra work. Be worth it. I hate working out without a team. . . .

Blackout.

End of ACT ONE.

Intermission, during which the "Suspended For Patriotism" article is distributed.

ACT TWO

SCENE ONE

SLIDE: "Sunday, April 1. 8:30 A.M. Phone Conversation between Dr. Seymour and Dr. Doane"

DR. ALBERT SEYMOUR and DR. GERTRUDE DOANE on opposite sides of the DC acting area. She is holding several sections of the newspaper.

DR. SEYMOUR: Gertrude, Al Seymour here. Did you see this morning's paper?

DR. DOANE: I was just reading it.

DR. SEYMOUR: Well, look at section D, page two. School News.

DR. GERTRUDE DOANE looks through the newspaper.

DR. DOANE: Oh, my!

DR. SEYMOUR: Is any of this true?

DR. DOANE: Al, the boy was not suspended because of singing the national anthem. He was

85

suspended because he was creating a disturbance. That's according to Joe.

DR. SEYMOUR: Joe?

DR. DOANE: Joe Palleni.

DR. SEYMOUR: Who is this Narwin woman?

DR. DOANE: An English teacher. A good teacher. She's been on the staff for years.

DR. SEYMOUR: Oh, yes. I think I know her. And that's all there is to it?

DR. DOANE: As far as I know. Al, no one could take this seriously.

DR. SEYMOUR: I hope not. With the budget vote soon . . . and the school board—

DR. DOANE: Do you want me to call the newspaper?

DR. SEYMOUR: Ah . . . no. But if you get any calls, refer them to me.

DR. DOANE: I will.

DR. SEYMOUR: This is not going to do us any good.

DR. DOANE: No one reads about schools.

DR. SEYMOUR: Let's hope so.

SLIDE: "9:20 A.M. Phone Conversation between Philip and Ken"

PHILIP MALLOY in UC acting area. KEN BARCHET in DC acting area.

PHILIP MALLOY: What's happening?

KEN BARCHET: Did you see today's paper?

PHILIP MALLOY: I deliver it. I don't read it.

KEN BARCHET: There's an article in it about you.

PHILIP MALLOY: Sure. April fool.

KEN BARCHET: No, really. Look at section D, page two.

PHILIP MALLOY: Right.

KEN BARCHET: It ain't true, but it's funny.

SLIDE: "9:50 A.M. Conversation between Philip Malloy's Parents"

SUSAN and BEN MALLOY in UC acting area. SUSAN MALLOY is looking through the newspaper. SLIDE: Kitchen wall.

SUSAN MALLOY: Look here, Ben. Here's the story about Philip.

BEN MALLOY: You're kidding! Let me see.

SUSAN MALLOY: Here.

BEN MALLOY takes the newspaper from SU-SAN MALLOY.

BEN MALLOY: I'll be. . . . See, the superintendent says there's no rule. It *was* just the teacher.

SUSAN MALLOY: It doesn't seem right.

BEN MALLOY: She should be fired. Is Philip around?

SUSAN MALLOY: I think so.

BEN MALLOY: Philip! Come in here and look at this.

PHILIP MALLOY enters UC acting area. SU-SAN MALLOY points out the article to PHILIP MALLOY.

BEN MALLOY: See? If you stick up for yourself, you get action. How's that make you feel? (*beat*) Philip?

SUSAN MALLOY: What's the matter?

PHILIP MALLOY: I don't know. Weird.

SUSAN MALLOY: It was the teacher. Just as you said.

BEN MALLOY: Just shows you—

SUSAN MALLOY: Where are you going?

PHILIP MALLOY: Upstairs.

PHILIP MALLOY exits.

SUSAN MALLOY: That Ted Griffen knows how to get things done.

BEN MALLOY: He gets my vote.

SLIDE: "2:30 P.M. Phone Conversation between Margaret Narwin and Her Sister"

MARGARET NARWIN in DC acting area.

MARGARET NARWIN: I just don't understand why they would ever print such a thing. (*pause*) But it's so slanted. And full of errors. (*pause*) Yes, I suppose you're right, people won't pay much attention to it. It's just. . . .

SLIDE: "7:30 P.M. Ted Griffen Delivers a Speech to a Meeting of the Harrison Sunday Fellowship"

TED GRIFFEN in SR acting area. SLIDE: Church assembly room.

TED GRIFFEN (*to the audience*): And if I am elected to the Harrison School Board, I will, one, keep the cost of education down to a reasonable level—which is to say that I will keep our taxes down—and two, I will work with the rest of the board to support basic American values. For I— and I can only speak for myself—I am shocked that a student should be suspended from one of our schools because he desires to sing the national anthem. Yes, my friends, it is true. This sad story is in today's *Record*. And, I say, what is the point of installing computers, which my generation never seemed to need, if our young people are not allowed to practice the elemental values of American patriotism?

SLIDE: "11:20 P.M. From the Diary of Philip Malloy"

PHILIP MALLOY in DC acting area. He is holding his diary.

PHILIP MALLOY (*to the audience*): Folks excited by the newspaper story. Dad keeps telling me how great I am. I wonder what will happen now. Maybe they'll kick Miss Narwin out. Wonder if she saw the article. It's her fault. Not mine. (*beat*) No one called. I guess I don't go to school tomorrow. (*beat*) Finished *The Outsiders*. Not bad. Wonder what it would be like to live without parents. You could do what you'd like.

SCENE TWO

SLIDE: "Monday, April 2. 8:05 A.M. The Jake Barlow Talk Show"

*JAKE BARLOW in SR acting area. SLIDE: Ra-
dio station studio.*

JAKE BARLOW: Okay. Okay. Here we go! All
sorts of things we can talk about. Wanting—and
waiting—to hear from you on WLRB, your
talk radio with your loudmouthed host Jake Barlow. Ready. Willing. And able! All kinds of
things going on. We can talk about that demonstration in Washington. I don't know about that.
Or that point-shaving scandal over at the university? Come on, guys, is that an education or
what?

Now here's a bit of a story that just came in
over the wires. Let me read it to you. Now, listen
up! This is America. I mean it! WLRB asking
you—Jake Barlow asking you—what you think
of *this*.

"Kicked out of school for patriotism."

Right, you heard me correct. I'm not making
this up. None of it. I'm *reading* it!

"Harrison." Where in the *world* is Harrison? In
the United States? In America? All their auto

91

plates read "Live free or die." Well, something died, because this is going on there right now! Here it is. Right in the morning news.

"A tenth-grader was suspended from his local school because he sang *The Star-Spangled Banner* during the school's morning exercises. The boy, Philip Malloy, who wished to sing in the spirit of patriotism, was then forced to remain at home alone, since both his parents work. English teacher Margaret Narwin, who brought about the suspension, maintains the boy was making a nuisance of himself."

Would you believe it? Okay, this is WLRB, all-talk radio. Take a short break, then come right back to talk about whatever you want. Man, but I'm telling you. What's happening to this country!

Now this. . . .

SLIDE: "8:07 A.M. Phone Conversation between Mrs. Gloria Harland, Chairperson, Harrison School Board, and Dr. Seymour"

MRS. GLORIA HARLAND and DR. ALBERT SEYMOUR on opposite sides of the DC acting area.

MRS. HARLAND: Albert, this is Gloria Harland. Good morning.

DR. SEYMOUR: Gloria! Good morning.

MRS. HARLAND: Al, last night I attended a meeting of the Harrison Sunday Fellowship—

DR. SEYMOUR: Oh, yes. Couldn't make it.

MRS. HARLAND: Well, Ted Griffen made a speech. He's running for the school board.

DR. SEYMOUR: Yes, right.

MRS. HARLAND: Albert, part of Ted's speech was an attack on the present board in regard to what he claims is the suspension of a student for singing the national anthem in one of the schools. One of the high schools, I think.

DR. SEYMOUR: Oh, Lord, is he going to make a thing about this?

MRS. HARLAND: What happened? It's not true, is it?

DR. SEYMOUR: I can assure you nothing of the kind occurred. Nothing. But let me make some further inquiries and then get back to you.

MRS. HARLAND: This is *not* what we need. Not with the budget vote so—

DR. SEYMOUR: Exactly, I understand.

SLIDE: "8:10 A.M. The Jack Barlow Talk Show"

JACK BARLOW in SR acting area. SLIDE: Radio station studio.

JACK BARLOW: Okay. Back again. And ready

to take you on. We've got the scandal at the university. The demonstration in Washington, D.C. The kid kicked out of school for being an American patriot. Anything you want. Here we go. First call. Hello?

CALLER #1 (*voice only*): Is this Jake?

JAKE BARLOW: Jake Cruising-for-a-Bruising Barlow. Who's this?

CALLER #1: This is Steve.

JAKE BARLOW: Steve! How you doing, big guy?

CALLER #1: Great. Look, about that kid.

JAKE BARLOW: The one kicked out of school?

CALLER #1: Yeah. That gripes me. Really does.

JAKE BARLOW: Right! What are schools for, anyway?

CALLER #1: People might call me a . . . a . . .

JAKE BARLOW: Jerk?

CALLER #1: Yeah, maybe. But like they used to say: America, love it or leave it. And that school—

JAKE BARLOW: It was a teacher.

CALLER #1: Yeah, teacher. She shouldn't be allowed to teach. That's my opinion.

JAKE BARLOW: Right. I'm with you there, Steve. I mean, there are the three R's—reading, 'riting, and 'rithmetic—and the three P's—prayer, patriotism, and parents. At least, that's my notion of schooling.

CALLER #1: Right. I'm right with you.

JAKE BARLOW: Okay, Steve. Like what you said. Let's see if we got any ultra-liberals out there who'll call in and try to defend this—I was about to say *woman*—person. Steve! Thanks for calling.

CALLER #1: Yeah.

JAKE BARLOW: Who's next?

SLIDE: "8:30 A.M. Conversation between Dr. Seymour and Dr. Doane"

DR. ALBERT SEYMOUR on DR. GERTRUDE DOANE on opposite sides of the DC acting area.

DR. SEYMOUR: Gert, Al here. Look, I just got a call from Gloria Harland about this boy who was suspended for singing.

DR. DOANE: Al, I told you, that's not why he was suspended.

DR. SEYMOUR: Maybe yes. Maybe no. But Gloria was at a meeting last night at which Ted Griffen claimed it's school policy to keep kids from singing—

DR. DOANE: That's absolutely untrue.

DR. SEYMOUR: It doesn't matter if it's true or not, Gert. What's important is what people are saying. Will be saying. I want a report on my desk. Make it short and to the point. Soon as you can.

DR. DOANE: Al—

DR. SEYMOUR: Gert, believe me. I'm sensitive to this sort of thing. Just do as I've requested.

SLIDE: "8:35 A.M. The Jake Barlow Talk Show"

JAKE BARLOW in SR acting area. SLIDE: Radio station studio.

JAKE BARLOW: Okay. Who's this?

CALLER #2 (*voice only*): My name is Liz.

JAKE BARLOW: Liz baby! How you doing?

CALLER #2: Just fine.

JAKE BARLOW: Liz, what's on your pretty mind this morning?

CALLER #2: Jake, I'm a mother. I have three kids. All school-age. But if I had a teacher like that—

JAKE BARLOW: Whoa! Back off. Like who?

CALLER #2: The one who forbade that child to show his patriotism. . . .

JAKE BARLOW: Right.

CALLER #2: I'd take my kids out of school.

JAKE BARLOW: You would? What about the teacher?

CALLER #2: Wouldn't let my kids go back unless she was removed.

JAKE BARLOW: The teacher doesn't have rights?

CALLER #2: It's a free country. But she has no right to do what she did. My husband was in the military. She's taking away rights.

JAKE BARLOW: Then you know.

CALLER #2: Yes, I do.

SLIDE: "9:17 A.M. Conversation between Robert Duval, Reporter for the *St. Louis Post-Dispatch*, and Dr. Doane"

ROBERT DUVAL and DR. GERTRUDE DOANE on opposite sides of the DC acting area.

ROBERT DUVAL: Is this Miss Doane, principal of Harrison High School?

DR. DOANE: Dr. Doane. Yes.

ROBERT DUVAL: Thank you. Of course. Dr. Doane, my name is Robert Duval. I'm a reporter with the *St. Louis Post-Dispatch*. I'm attempting to follow up on an AAP release that indicates your school suspended a student because he sang *The Star-Spangled Banner*.

DR. DOANE: Did you say St. Louis?

ROBERT DUVAL: Yes, ma'am. Missouri. Took the story off the wire service. And we ran it. Now you see, we have our state American Legion convention going on here. Someone noticed the item and called to see if we had any more information.

DR. DOANE: Are you serious?

ROBERT DUVAL: Certainly am.

DR. DOANE: Is it being sent out over the whole country?

ROBERT DUVAL: Well, actually, it has been sent out. Would you like to comment, ma'am?

DR. DOANE: There has been some mistake, and . . . None of this is true.

ROBERT DUVAL: None of it? The boy was not suspended, then?

DR. DOANE: Yes, suspended, but not for those reasons. Look, Mr. Duval, I have to sort this out.

ROBERT DUVAL: When can I call back?

DR. DOANE: Give me a few hours.

ROBERT DUVAL: Yes, ma'am.

SLIDE: "9:32 A.M. The Jake Barlow Talk Show"

JAKE BARLOW in the SR acting area. SLIDE: Radio station studio.

JAKE BARLOW: Back again. Who's on?

CALLER #3 (*voice only*): This is Roger.

JAKE BARLOW: Roger Rabbit?

CALLER #3: Not quite.

JAKE BARLOW: How many kids do you have?

CALLER #3: Ah . . . two.

JAKE BARLOW: Get hopping, Roger, get hopping. Ha! Okay, Roger, what's on your mind?

CALLER #3: About all these calls about the boy who was kicked out.

JAKE BARLOW: Makes me sick. *Sick!*

CALLER #3: Well, you've read the story a few times, so I think I understand it. And it seems to me that couldn't be the whole story.

JAKE BARLOW: What do you mean?

CALLER #3: Well, the story is slanted from the point of view of the boy. It doesn't really indicate what the teacher's position is.

JAKE BARLOW: Roger—let me get this right— you are defending this so-called teacher?

CALLER #3: No, I don't say that. But the story you read is the boy's, not the teacher's. Why should we assume that the teacher is wrong?

JAKE BARLOW: Come on. Give us a break. The kid was suspended, right?

CALLER #3: So it would appear.

JAKE BARLOW: Suspended for singing the national anthem, right?

CALLER #3: That's the story you read.

JAKE BARLOW: Now, how could singing the national anthem ever . . . *ever* be making a nuisance?

CALLER #3: Well . . .

JAKE BARLOW: Roger, what's your point? Let me guess. You're a teacher!

CALLER #3: Actually, I'm a salesman.

JAKE BARLOW: What do you sell?

CALLER #3: That doesn't make—

JAKE BARLOW: Come on! Out with it!

CALLER #3: Well, books, but—

JAKE BARLOW: Yeah, see? Exactly. And here you are defending this *creep* of a teacher. What does the kid know other than his own, natural-born patriotism? And then this teacher comes along and squelches it. And this country has all these problems with morality, drugs, pornography. No way, José.

CALLER #3: But—

JAKE BARLOW: Good-bye! Always one rotten apple. Hey, out there. Do you agree with this guy? Tell you what! Why don't we start a crusade. I want you all to write to the teacher. Hey, free country! Do you agree with what she did?

Okay, tell her. If you disagree, tell her that. Let's see, here's her name. Margaret Narwin. N—a—r—w—i—n. Just write her. Postcard. *Brick*. Hey, just kidding. Okay! Now this . . .

SLIDE: "10:00 A.M. Conversation between Dr. Doane, Margaret Narwin, and Dr. Palleni"

DR. GERTRUDE DOANE, MARGARET NARWIN, and DR. JOSEPH PALLENI are in the SL acting area. SLIDE: Classroom wall.

DR. DOANE: I know you're upset, but I have to get it down clearly. Peg, just tell me what happened. We all need to tell the same story.

DR. PALLENI: Amen. Gert's trying to be helpful, Peg.

MARGARET NARWIN: It's terribly unsettling.

DR. DOANE: Well, yes . . . to all of us. Now, once more. Please.

MARGARET NARWIN: Very well. Philip Malloy, from the first day he entered my homeroom last week . . . during the time the students are asked to stand in silence—

DR. PALLENI: The rule is "respectful silence." It's in your memo about opening exercises. Isn't in the student handbook. But I think it should be.

102

DR. DOANE: Good point.

MARGARET NARWIN: During the playing of the national anthem, he sang. Loudly. To make a commotion. Obviously. The first time he did it, I asked him to stop, and he did. After a bit. The second two times, he didn't. He refused. That's when I sent him to Joe.

DR. PALLENI: The boy admitted it, Gert.

MARGARET NARWIN: Deliberately provocative.

DR. DOANE: Do we know why, Peg?

MARGARET NARWIN: I haven't the slightest idea.

DR. DOANE: Joe?

DR. PALLENI: Nope. No problems before. Ever.

DR. DOANE: Maybe I should talk to some students.

MARGARET NARWIN: He's always been restless in English class. Sort of a wise guy. I don't know why. In his last exam he wrote a very foolish answer. Mocking me.

DR. DOANE: You?

MARGARET NARWIN: Oh, yes. Absolutely. Mocking.

DR. DOANE: Do you still have it?

MARGARET NARWIN: I always return exams to students.

DR. DOANE: Too bad. But there must be some reason. . . .

MARGARET NARWIN: I agree.

DR. PALLENI: Home, Gert. Ninety-nine point nine times out of a hundred, you get a thing like this, a kid acting out, believe me, it's home.

DR. DOANE: But we don't know that.

DR. PALLENI: Hey, what's the difference? The parents always blame the school.

DR. DOANE: As far as I'm concerned, this is strictly a discipline problem. That's what I intend to tell people. Do you agree?

DR. PALLENI: Well, the thing is, it's the truth.

MARGARET NARWIN: I don't think it was wise to suspend him.

DR. PALLENI: Two infractions in one week, Peg. That's the rule. If we start breaking the rules each time—

DR. DOANE: Joe, draft something—keep it strictly to the facts—to give to Seymour. Do it immediately. I want to speak to some students.

SLIDE: "11:00 A.M. From the Drafted Memo Written by Dr. Palleni"

DR. JOSEPH PALLENI in DC acting area.

DR. PALLENI: Three. On March twenty-eighth, twenty-ninth, and thirtieth, Philip Malloy caused a disturbance in his homeroom class (Margaret Narwin, teacher) by singing the national anthem in a loud, raucous, *disrespectful* manner.

Four. When asked by Miss Narwin on the first occasion to cease, Philip Malloy reluctantly did so. But on the second and third occasions, he refused and was sent to Assistant Principal Joe Palleni for discipline.

Five. Philip Malloy does not dispute the above facts.

Six. On the third occurrence, Philip Malloy was asked to promise not to show such a disrespectful attitude, and to apologize to the teacher and his fellow classmates. *He refused*.

SLIDE: "11:15 A.M. Conversation between Dr. Doane and Ken Barchet"

DR. GERTRUDE DOANE and KEN BARCHET in SR acting area. SLIDE: Office wall.

DR. DOANE: Ken, I'm just trying to understand what happened there. Is this clear?

KEN BARCHET: Yes.

DR. DOANE: I hope you can speak freely. In your view—what occurred?

KEN BARCHET: Well, you know, the music went on—

DR. DOANE: Which day was this?

KEN BARCHET: Wednesday.

DR. DOANE: Okay.

KEN BARCHET: Right. The music went on. And we were just standing there. And the next thing, Miss Narwin was telling Philip to stop.

DR. DOANE: Stop what?

KEN BARCHET: I'm not sure. The newspaper said singing.

DR. DOANE: What about the other days?

KEN BARCHET: You know, he was, again . . . sort of, I guess . . . singing.

DR. DOANE: In what way?

KEN BARCHET: Just singing.

DR. DOANE: Loudly?

KEN BARCHET: Not really.

DR. DOANE: But you heard him?

KEN BARCHET: I guess.

DR. DOANE: How close to Philip do you sit?

KEN BARCHET: Across the room.

DR. DOANE: So, loudly enough for you to hear?

KEN BARCHET: Well . . .

DR. DOANE: Then what happened?

KEN BARCHET: Miss Narwin got mad.

DR. DOANE: Why?

KEN BARCHET: Well, you know . . . like you said . . . Philip was singing. And I guess we're not supposed to.

DR. DOANE: Did Philip stop?

KEN BARCHET: Yeah. When she told him to get out.

DR. DOANE: Not before?

KEN BARCHET: No.

DR. DOANE: What did the class do?

KEN BARCHET: I wasn't paying attention.

KEN BARCHET in SL acting area. PHILIP MALLOY in UC acting area. SLIDE: School hallway.

KEN BARCHET: Hey, man, what's happening?

PHILIP MALLOY: Nothing. What's happening there?

KEN BARCHET: Just spoke to Doane.

PHILIP MALLOY: How come?

KEN BARCHET: She called me in to find out what happened.

PHILIP MALLOY: What did you tell her?

KEN BARCHET: What happened. The whole thing. Lot of people talking about it.

PHILIP MALLOY: Yeah, but what did you tell her?

KEN BARCHET: I thought I should tell her how funny it was.

PHILIP MALLOY: Come on! What?

KEN BARCHET: Nothing. I mean, it wasn't anything. I don't know why they're making a fuss about it.

PHILIP MALLOY: I still have English with Narwin, but they switched me back to Lunser's homeroom.

KEN BARCHET: He's okay. Tells good jokes. Someone told me he has a collection of joke books. That's where he gets all those one-liners. (*beat*) We going to work out this afternoon?

PHILIP MALLOY: Yeah.

KEN BARCHET: Catch you later.

SLIDE: "11:50 A.M. Conversation between Dr. Doane and Cynthia Gambia, Student"

DR. GERTRUDE DOANE and CYNTHIA GAMBIA in SR acting area. SLIDE: Office wall.

DR. DOANE: Cynthia, I'm trying to find out what happened in Miss Narwin's homeroom class. With Philip Malloy.

CYNTHIA GAMBIA: Yes, I understand. I wasn't paying much attention.

DR. DOANE: That's all right. Just tell me what happened as you saw it.

CYNTHIA GAMBIA: Well, during *The Star-Spangled Banner*, when the tape went on, Philip started to hum.

DR. DOANE: *Hum?*

CYNTHIA GAMBIA: I think so.

DR. DOANE: Not sing?

CYNTHIA GAMBIA: It could have been. I wasn't paying attention. Not at first.

DR. DOANE: And then?

CYNTHIA GAMBIA: Miss Narwin asked him to leave.

DR. DOANE: Which days were these?

CYNTHIA GAMBIA: All three.

DR. DOANE: Was Philip causing a disturbance?

CYNTHIA GAMBIA: Well, I heard him. I mean, it wasn't loud or anything. Not like the paper said. But he wouldn't stop. And she did ask him. I guess that was the disturbance.

DR. DOANE: So he wasn't loud.

CYNTHIA GAMBIA: Maybe the last time.

DR. DOANE: What day was that?

CYNTHIA GAMBIA: Ah ... I'm not sure. Wednesday? Thursday?

DR. DOANE: What did the other students do?

CYNTHIA GAMBIA: Nothing.

DR. DOANE: Do you have any idea why Philip did this?

CYNTHIA GAMBIA: No.

DR. DOANE: Do you want to add anything?

CYNTHIA GAMBIA: No. I guess not. I mean, he *was* being sort of rude.

DR. DOANE: Philip?

CYNTHIA GAMBIA: Miss Narwin did ask him to stop. You're supposed to be quiet. Everybody says that's the rule. He certainly wasn't. She's a fair teacher. All the kids say so.

SLIDE: "12:30 P.M. Ted Griffen Delivers a Speech to the Harrison Rotary Club"

TED GRIFFIN in DC acting area.

TED GRIFFIN (*to the audience*): And, if elected, I will work with the rest of the board to support basic American values. I am shocked that a Harrison student should be expelled from one of our schools simply because he desires to sing the national anthem. What is the point of installing computers if our young people are not allowed to practice the elemental values of American patriotism? Is that the way we budget our education dollars?

SLIDE: "12:50 P.M. Conversation between Dr. Doane and Allison Doresett"

DR. GERTRUDE DOANE and ALLISON DORESETT in SR acting area. SLIDE: Office wall.

DR. DOANE: Now, as I understand it, you are in Miss Narwin's homeroom class. So you were there all three times?

ALLISON DORESETT: Uh-huh.

DR. DOANE: Tell me what you saw.

ALLISON DORESETT: Well, Philip, he doesn't like Miss Narwin.

DR. DOANE: Do you know why?

ALLISON DORESETT: It's what people are saying. In English class he just sits there, like he's bored and can't stand anything she says. It's just the way he looks. But then he suddenly makes some remark, a joke or something. Something funny.

DR. DOANE: Do you think this has anything to do with what happened?

ALLISON DORESETT: Well, it was so obvious he was trying to get at her.

DR. DOANE: What do you mean?

ALLISON DORESETT: Get her mad.

DR. DOANE: Because he doesn't like her?

ALLISON DORESETT: I think he was doing it to get Miss Narwin in trouble.

DR. DOANE: I wish you'd tell me more.

ALLISON DORESETT: Well, he's been angry a lot lately. I go home on the same bus with him. The other day I—you know—tried to sit next to him. On the bus. He wouldn't talk to me.

DR. DOANE: Do you know why?

ALLISON DORESETT: That's the way he is.

DR. DOANE: Allison, I appreciate your help.

ALLISON DORESETT: Can I say something?

DR. DOANE: Of course.

ALLISON DORESETT: I like Miss Narwin.

DR. DOANE: I'm glad. Your telling the truth can only help her.

SLIDE: "1:30 P.M. Memo to Dr. Seymour as Re-written by Dr. Doane"

DR. GERTRUDE DOANE in SR acting area.
SLIDE: Office wall.

DR. DOANE: Three. On March twenty-eighth, twenty-ninth, and thirtieth Philip Malloy deliberately caused a disturbance in his homeroom class (Margaret Narwin, teacher) by singing the national anthem in a loud, raucous, *disrespectful* fashion, thereby drawing attention to himself.

Four. When requested by Miss Narwin on the first occasion to cease, Philip Malloy did so, albeit reluctantly. On the second and third occasions, he repeated his disrespectful behavior, and when he refused to stop, he was sent—standard procedure—to Assistant Principal Dr. Joseph Palleni for discipline.

Five. Philip Malloy did not dispute the above facts.

Six. A random selection of students who were in the classroom at the time confirms these events. Indeed, there is evidence that Philip Malloy's acts were indicative of some personal animosity he feels toward the homeroom teacher, Miss Narwin. His rudeness was also on display in the English classes he had with her. His grade there indicates inferior work.

Seven. On the third occurrence, Philip Malloy was asked to: one) promise not to show such a disrespectful attitude toward our national anthem and, two) apologize to his teacher and his classmates for his behavior. He refused, choosing the option afforded him of suspension.

SLIDE: "2:22 P.M. Telegrams"

JESSICA WITTINGTON, HANK MORGAN, and CHARLES ELDERSON in DC acting area.

114

JESSICA WITTINGTON (*to the audience*): Telegram to Margaret Narwin, Harrison High School. From Young Americans for America. "On behalf of our membership we strongly condemn your suppression of patriotism in the American school system. Sincerely, Jessica Wittington, Executive Secretary, Tampa, Florida."

HANK MORGAN (*to the audience*): Telegram to Philip Malloy. From the Society for the Preservation of Free Speech. "We applaud your defense of the freedom of speech in a public arena. One is never too young to fight for our constitutional rights, which are under constant assault from right-wing forces. Stand firm. Stand tall. Please call us for active support. Hank Morgan, Chicago, Illinois."

CHARLES ELDERSON (*to the audience*): Telegram to Principal, Harrison High. "People like Margaret Narwin should be kicked out of teaching. Charles Elderson, Woodbank, North Carolina."

SLIDE: "3:30 P.M. Memo to Mrs. Gloria Harland from Dr. Seymour"

DR. ALBERT SEYMOUR in SR acting area. SLIDE: Office wall.

DR. SEYMOUR: Three. On March twenty-eighth, twenty-ninth, and thirtieth, Philip Malloy deliberately caused a disturbance in his homeroom class (Margaret Narwin, a teacher of twenty years' standing) by singing the national anthem in a loud, raucous, *disrespectful* fashion, thereby drawing attention to himself and away from the words. There are strong indications that he was acting out some personal animosity toward the teacher in question for reasons unknown. His school performance has been inferior. (It has been suggested that there may be problems in the home area. Please note, however, that the law *requires* schools to keep such personal information confidential.)

Four. When requested by his teacher, Miss Narwin, on the first occasion to maintain a dignified response to the national anthem, Philip Malloy did so, though reluctantly. On the second and third occasions, he repeated his disrespectful acts, and when he refused to stop, he was—as a matter of course—sent to Assistant Principal Dr. Joseph Palleni for discipline.

Five. Philip Malloy, when given the opportunity, did *not* dispute the above facts.

Six. Students who were in the classroom at the time of the incidents confirm these events.

Seven. On the third occurrence, Philip Malloy was requested to: one) promise that he would show an attitude of respect toward our national anthem, and two) apologize to his teacher and his classmates for his rude behavior. He refused, choosing the option of suspension *himself*.

SLIDE: "6:20 P.M. Conversation between Philip Malloy's Parents"

SUSAN and BEN MALLOY in UC acting area.
SLIDE: Kitchen wall.

BEN MALLOY: Hi! Where's Philip?

SUSAN MALLOY: He just got in. Washing up.

BEN MALLOY: People were talking about him today. Amazing how many folks saw that thing in the paper.

SUSAN MALLOY: At my place, too.

BEN MALLOY: Makes you feel good.

SUSAN MALLOY: We should celebrate.

PHILIP MALLOY enters.

BEN MALLOY: Well, how do you feel?

PHILIP MALLOY: Okay.

SUSAN MALLOY: You should be pleased with yourself.

BEN MALLOY: What do you think of all the telegrams?

PHILIP MALLOY: I don't know. Who are those people? I never heard of them before.

BEN MALLOY: They've heard of you. You're famous. Just shows you. One person, standing up for what he believes in, makes a difference.

SUSAN MALLOY: I'm just so glad it's worked out all right. Aren't you?

PHILIP MALLOY: I suppose.

BEN MALLOY: What's the problem now?

PHILIP MALLOY: It'll be weird going back. What kids will say.

BEN MALLOY: They'll be on your side. Just make sure you sing in the morning. People will look to that.

PHILIP MALLOY: I'll be in Mr. Lunser's class.

BEN MALLOY: You said he likes kids singing.

PHILIP MALLOY: Sort of.

BEN MALLOY: I think you should go over and speak to Ted Griffen, too.

PHILIP MALLOY: Why?

BEN MALLOY: Someone at work heard him at some speech he gave—the school board thing— he mentioned this whole business. . . .

PHILIP MALLOY: He did?

SUSAN MALLOY: And he brought in that reporter.

BEN MALLOY: Come on, Philip, people are really on your side!

PHILIP MALLOY: I guess.

SLIDE: "7:30 P.M. Ted Griffen Delivers a Speech to a Meeting of the Harrison Chamber of Commerce"

TED GRIFFEN in SR acting area. SLIDE: Meeting room.

TED GRIFFEN (*to the audience*): I am a great believer in basic American values. But what I say is—most emphatically—what is the point of installing computers if our young people are not allowed to practice the elemental values of American patriotism? And to think—because this story has been picked up by the national press—how shocking it is that this is the way our town of Harrison should come to be known. It should not be condoned!

SLIDE: "8:10 P.M. Phone Conversation between Margaret Narwin and Dr. Gertrude Doane"

MARGARET NARWIN and DR. GERTRUDE DOANE on opposite sides of DC acting area.

DR. DOANE: Yes, Peg, hello. How are you?

MARGARET NARWIN: Gert, I . . .

119

DR. DOANE: Peg, are you all right?

MARGARET NARWIN: Gert, I just got a call from my sister in Florida . . . about a newspaper story—

DR. DOANE: I know, Peg. I've already heard about it. I just didn't see any point in upsetting you any more.

MARGARET NARWIN: But why?

DR. DOANE: I already received a call from some midwestern reporter. There have been telegrams—

MARGARET NARWIN: Telegrams?

DR. DOANE: At school. I told the office to hold them. Peg, it's gotten out of hand.

MARGARET NARWIN: I want to see them. What do the telegrams say?

DR. DOANE: Well, they believe what the story says and—

MARGARET NARWIN: Were they addressed to me?

DR. DOANE: Well, to me, and yes, some to you, but—

MARGARET NARWIN: I want to see them.

DR. DOANE: Peg, I assure you, I have complete confidence in you.

MARGARET NARWIN: It's so monstrous, so . . .

DR. DOANE: Peg, we're just going to have to weather it and . . . maybe you'll want to take the day off tomorrow.

MARGARET NARWIN: No, I can't give in to this—

DR. DOANE: Peg, believe me. It will calm down.

SLIDE: "10:33 P.M. From the Diary of Philip Malloy"

PHILIP MALLOY in UC acting area. He is holding his diary.

PHILIP MALLOY (*to the audience*): Weird day not doing much. Got these telegrams from people I never heard of before, talking about something I didn't get. Folks all high. Be glad to be back in school. I hate sitting around. Glad to be in Lunser's homeroom class again. Get things back to normal. Guess I'll still be in Narwin's English. Better speak to her and see if I can do some extra work. So I can get on the track team. Wonder what she'll say? (*beat*) Did some extra time on Dad's rowing machine. (*beat*) I'm a little nervous.

SCENE THREE

SLIDE: "Tuesday, April third. Letters sent to Margaret Narwin"

CARLTON HAVEN, DAVID MAIK, and LAURA JACOBS in DC acting area.

CARLTON HAVEN (*to the audience*): "Dear Margaret Narwin. As a teacher in the Dayton, Ohio school system for ten years, I am dismayed and horrified that in this day and age a colleague of mine should suspend a student from school for singing the national anthem. We suffer enough from unfair criticism. The profession does not need people like you who make it so hard for the rest of us. Carlton Haven."

DAVID MAIK (*to the audience*): "Margaret Narwin. I'm a veteran who fought for this country and gave his blood and I really hate people like you. David Maik, Eugene, Oregon."

LAURA JACOBS (*to the audience*): "Margaret Narwin. It seems to me that people like you, who don't believe in patriotism, cause the problems. Surely you have something better to do with your classroom authority than attacking kids who express their love of our country. Or maybe you should find a better profession for your lack of ability. Laura Jacobs, San Diego, California."

SLIDE: "7:15 A.M. Conversation between Dr. Seymour and Dr. Doane in the Superintendent's Office"

DR. ALBERT SEYMOUR and DR. GERTRUDE DOANE in SR acting area. They are each holding a number of telegrams.

DR. DOANE: How many are there?

DR. SEYMOUR: Telegrams. Ten. Fifteen. Every one of them demanding we fire this Narwin woman.

DR. DOANE: Not this one.

DR. SEYMOUR: Well, the overwhelming majority. And I had twelve calls at my home last night.

DR. DOANE: From whom?

DR. SEYMOUR: People in town. People who vote. They're outraged.

DR. DOANE: And they believe that story. . . .

DR. SEYMOUR: I'm beginning to believe it.

DR. DOANE: Al!

DR. SEYMOUR: What do you expect me to do?

DR. DOANE: I expect you to support Peg Narwin.

DR. SEYMOUR: A TV network wants to interview people.

DR. DOANE: You're not going to let them. . . .

DR. SEYMOUR: No. No. But the board wants me to issue a statement. Gert, I have an appointment with this Ted Griffen at nine-fifteen.

DR. DOANE: Griffen is running for board. . . .

DR. SEYMOUR: Exactly. He's already made speeches about this business. Look, Gert, I'm sorry, but between you and me—quote me and I'll deny it—I don't care about the board. I can handle them. But the budget . . . if we lose again . . .

DR. DOANE: I know.

DR. SEYMOUR: People scream if kids are not educated. Then they scream if you ask them for the money to do it.

DR. DOANE: Yes, I know.

DR. SEYMOUR: I want to see the file on Narwin.

DR. DOANE: Why?

DR. SEYMOUR: I have to decide what to do.

DR. DOANE: Before your meeting with this Griffen?

DR. SEYMOUR: Exactly.

SLIDE: "7:30 A.M. Conversation between Philip and His Parents During Breakfast"

PHILIP MALLOY plus SUSAN and BEN MALLOY in UC acting area. SLIDE: Kitchen wall.

BEN MALLOY: You don't have to be nervous about anything. You were right. The fact that they moved you out of that woman's class proves you were right.

PHILIP MALLOY: Just homeroom. I still have English with her.

SUSAN MALLOY: I'm sure she won't give you any more trouble.

PHILIP MALLOY: It's just the other kids . . .

BEN MALLOY: You said they hated her, too.

PHILIP MALLOY: Yeah. . . .

SUSAN MALLOY: Do you want me to drive you?

PHILIP MALLOY: I'm meeting Ken.

SUSAN MALLOY: You'll be fine.

BEN MALLOY: As I've told you, half your runs are won at the start. Leap out of the blocks. Show them what you can do.

PHILIP MALLOY: Easy for you—

SUSAN MALLOY: Phil, you better go if you don't want to miss your bus.

SLIDE: "7:40 A.M. Conversation between Philip and Ken on the Way to the School Bus"

PHILIP MALLOY and KEN BARCHET in DC acting area.

PHILIP MALLOY: What's happening?

KEN BARCHET: Nothing. What's with you?

PHILIP MALLOY: Not much. We going to run this afternoon?

KEN BARCHET: Can't. Got track team right after school. Coach told us it's going to be at least three hours. You really should have tried out, man. You know that Polanski kid?

PHILIP MALLOY: Brian?

126

KEN BARCHET: Right. Coach has him down for the four hundred.

PHILIP MALLOY: Can't do anything.

KEN BARCHET: Best we got. (*beat*) You mad at the coach or something?

PHILIP MALLOY: No. Why?

KEN BARCHET: You should change your mind about being on the team.

PHILIP MALLOY: Yeah, I might. (*beat*) Want to know why I didn't go out? Narwin.

KEN BARCHET: What did she have to do with it?

PHILIP MALLOY: She almost flunked me in English. That meant I wasn't allowed to try out.

KEN BARCHET: That's why you're mad at her?

PHILIP MALLOY: But I'm going to ask her if I can do extra work. For credit.

KEN BARCHET: Think she'll give it to you?

PHILIP MALLOY: I don't know. I'll ask.

KEN BARCHET: Be great if you could get on the team.

PHILIP MALLOY: That's what I've been thinking.

SLIDE: "7:45 A.M. Conversation between Margaret Narwin and Dr. Doane"

MARGARET NARWIN and DR. GERTRUDE DOANE in SR acting area. A mail bag full of letters sits beside the desk. SLIDE: Office wall.

MARGARET NARWIN: I don't believe it!

DR. DOANE: It is incredible.

MARGARET NARWIN: How many telegrams are there?

DR. DOANE: Here? Almost two hundred. (*beat*) The superintendent's office put out a statement explaining the true situation.

MARGARET NARWIN: What did he say? May I see it?

DR. DOANE: Of course. Here.

DR. GERTRUDE DOANE hands MARGARET NARWIN the statement, which she reads.

DR. DOANE: What's the matter?

MARGARET NARWIN: This doesn't support me. I pleaded with Joe not to suspend him.

DR. DOANE: Peg, it does.

MARGARET NARWIN: Where?

DR. DOANE: Peg, understand that. . . . I need to tell you I said no to some TV people.

MARGARET NARWIN: No. Absolutely not.

DR. DOANE: Exactly. They can't come in without permission. Peg, do you want to take the day off?

MARGARET NARWIN: No. They'll come to my home. (*beat*) Gert, I don't understand. I have been teaching—

DR. DOANE: People believe what they read.

MARGARET NARWIN (*looking at her watch*): I have my class. . . .

DR. DOANE: Peg, I've moved Philip from your English class. He's with Mr. Keegan.

MARGARET NARWIN (*surprised*): Gert, people will misconstrue.

DR. DOANE: We are trying to be even-handed. . . .

MARGARET NARWIN: He's a student. I'm a teacher. Hands are not meant to be even.

DR. DOANE: That's my decision.

SLIDE: "7:55 A.M. Conversation between Philip and Allison"

PHILIP MALLOY and ALLISON DORESETT in DC acting area.

ALLISON DORESETT: Philip!

PHILIP MALLOY: Oh, hi.

ALLISON DORESETT: I just want you to know that I think what you did was really mean.

PHILIP MALLOY: What?

ALLISON DORESETT: Narwin is one of the best teachers. All the kids say so. It's really embarrassing.

PHILIP MALLOY: What are you talking about?

ALLISON DORESETT: You were just doing that to annoy her.

PHILIP MALLOY: Who?

ALLISON DORESETT: Miss Narwin. Everybody knows it. She's so fair.

ALLISON DORESETT exits.

PHILIP MALLOY: That's not true.

SLIDE: "8:03 A.M. Discussion in Bernard Lunser's Homeroom Class"

BERNARD LUNSER, PHILIP MALLOY, STUDENT #1, and STUDENT #2 in SL acting area. SLIDE (the one used at the beginning of Scene Two): Classroom wall.

BERNARD LUNSER: Let's go! Let's go! Seats. My God, it's Philip Malloy, Harrison High's own Uncle Sam. Take any empty seat, Philip. I'll set it later.

INTERCOM (*voice of Dr. Gertrude Doane*): Good morning to all students, faculty, and staff. Today is Tuesday, April third. Today will be a Schedule B day.

BERNARD LUNSER: That's B for bozos, boys and girls. B!

INTERCOM: Today in history. On this day, in the year thirteen-sixty-six, King Henry the Fourth of England was born.

BERNARD LUNSER: Not to be confused with a fifth of scotch.

INTERCOM: In nineteen-sixty-one, actor Eddie Murphy was born.

BERNARD LUNSER: My only competition.

INTERCOM: Please all rise and stand at respectful, silent attention for the playing of our national anthem.

BERNARD LUNSER: Philip!

PHILIP MALLOY: What?

BERNARD LUNSER: You want to sing?

STUDENTS: Yeah, sing!

BERNARD LUNSER: Keep your lip buttoned, Brian! Philip?

PHILIP MALLOY: No. . . .

BERNARD LUNSER: Okay. Just making sure your rights are protected.

**Oh, say can you see by the dawn's early light,
What so proudly we hailed at the twilight's last gleaming?**

BERNARD LUNSER: You sure, Philip?

PHILIP MALLOY: Yeah. . . .

**Whose broad stripes and bright stars, thro' the perilous fight,
O'er the ramparts we watched were so gallantly streaming? . . .**

SLIDE: "Letters sent to Philip Malloy"

ROLANDO MERCHAUD, MS. HARBOR, and AMERICAN LEGIONNAIRE in DC acting area.

ROLANDO MERCHAUD (*to the audience*): "Dear Philip. We support your defense of America. Keep on singing. We all join in. Rolando Merchaud, Red Oak, Iowa."

MS. HARBOR (*to the audience*): "Dear Philip. We, Ms. Harbor's fourth grade class at the Robert Fulton School, like to sing *The Star-Spangled Banner*, too. You can come to our school. Ms. Harbor's fourth grade class, Robert Fulton School, Brooklyn, New York."

AMERICAN LEGIONNAIRE (*to the audience*): "To Philip Malloy. American Legion Post number sixteen of Newport, Rhode Island salutes you for your defense of American values. Fight the good fight. Thumbs-up!"

SLIDE: "8:16 A.M. Conversations between Philip and Students in the Hallway on the Way to First Class"

PHILIP MALLOY, TODD BECKER, STUDENT #2, and STUDENT #3 in SL acting area. SLIDE: School hallway.

TODD BECKER: Hey, Philip, what's happening, man?

PHILIP MALLOY: Nothing.

TODD BECKER: You going to have a press conference?

PHILIP MALLOY: Get off!

STUDENT #2: Look out! Here comes Uncle Sam! That's what Mr. Lunser called him.

STUDENT #3: What's it like to be famous, newspapers and all?

PHILIP MALLOY: Come on. I have to get to class.

TODD BECKER: Oh, let the big man go.

STUDENT #3: Hey, Philip? How come you went after Narwin? I heard it was because you were failing English! That true?

PHILIP MALLOY: I have a class!

PHILIP MALLOY exits.

STUDENT #2: Let Uncle Sam go.

SLIDE: "9:20 A.M. Conversation between Dr. Seymour and Ted Griffen"

DR. ALBERT SEYMOUR and TED GRIFFEN in SR acting area. SLIDE: Office wall.

DR. SEYMOUR: Mr. Griffen. Nice to meet you. Come right in.

TED GRIFFEN: Thank you.

DR. SEYMOUR: Get you some coffee?

TED GRIFFEN: No, thanks.

DR. SEYMOUR: Look, Mr. Griffen—

TED GRIFFEN: Call me Ted.

DR. SEYMOUR: Fine. Ted. I'm Al. I've heard you speak a couple of times . . . was very interested in what you had to say. . . . I thought it would be a good idea, generally, to meet you. Sort of talk things over.

TED GRIFFEN: I appreciate that, Al.

DR. SEYMOUR: Now, what we've got here . . . well, the media . . . they never pay attention to us unless something bad—

TED GRIFFEN: Right. I never trust anything that's in print.

DR. SEYMOUR: Exactly. But we've got these elections coming up . . . budget.

TED GRIFFEN: And the board.

DR. SEYMOUR: Exactly. I'm prepared to work with anyone who's on the board. . . . But the budget thing—

TED GRIFFEN: Have to keep costs down.

DR. SEYMOUR: Absolutely. But, Ted, I'll be frank with you. All this publicity—negative publicity—won't do us any good.

TED GRIFFEN: I understand.

DR. SEYMOUR: That first budget was tight. And this second budget . . . to the bone. Get any closer and we're scooping marrow. Now, I understand no one wants to pay a cent more. But without that budget, education is in big trouble here in Harrison.

TED GRIFFEN: People want to hold the line on taxes.

DR. SEYMOUR: I sympathize. I pay taxes, too. But there's been a real misunderstanding regarding this national anthem thing. Let me share some facts with you. We have *no* rule against singing the national anthem. Never have had. Never will.

TED GRIFFEN: But the boy was suspended.

DR. SEYMOUR: Just getting to that. What I suspect here . . . we've got a personal problem.

TED GRIFFEN: With the boy? He seems—

DR. SEYMOUR: Now, Ted, I'm speaking in confidence.

TED GRIFFEN: Sure.

DR. SEYMOUR: Then we understand. It's not the boy. It's the teacher.

TED GRIFFEN: Well, I thought . . . what kind of a problem?

DR. SEYMOUR: Let me quote from a letter she wrote just a few weeks ago to her principal. I can't give you a copy, you understand, but I can read part of it to you . . . so you can understand what I'm up against.

TED GRIFFEN: Sure.

DR. SEYMOUR: She says here, and I'm quoting her, "The truth is . . . I feel that sometimes I am a little out of touch with contemporary teaching, and, just as important, the students who come before me." In other words, she's been around since history began.

TED GRIFFEN: Oh, boy. You've got a problem there.

DR. SEYMOUR: Exactly. The question is, what are you and I going to do about it?

SLIDE: "1:30 P.M. Conversation between Philip and Margaret Narwin"

PHILIP MALLOY and MARGARET NARWIN in SL acting area. SLIDE: Classroom wall.

PHILIP MALLOY: Miss Narwin?

MARGARET NARWIN: Philip? What are you doing here? What do you want?

PHILIP MALLOY: My class.

MARGARET NARWIN: You're . . . you're not in this section anymore. You were switched.

PHILIP MALLOY: I was?

MARGARET NARWIN: You're in Mr. Keegan's class.

PHILIP MALLOY: But . . .

MARGARET NARWIN: What?

PHILIP MALLOY: To get my grade up . . . I was going to ask for extra work. . . .

MARGARET NARWIN: Philip, you are no longer in my class.

PHILIP MALLOY: So I could get on the track team and . . .

MARGARET NARWIN: You are *not* in my class.

PHILIP MALLOY: But what about the grade?

MARGARET NARWIN: Please leave the room.

PHILIP MALLOY: But—

MARGARET NARWIN: Go!

PHILIP MALLOY: I'm leaving.

MARGARET NARWIN: Speak to Dr. Doane.

SLIDE: "2:50 P.M. Conversation between Philip
and Coach Earl Jamison"

*PHILIP MALLOY and COACH JAMISON in
SR acting area.*

PHILIP MALLOY: Can I talk to you a minute?

COACH JAMISON: Yeah. Sure.

PHILIP MALLOY: Remember, you said I should
ask Miss Narwin for some extra work. . . .

COACH JAMISON: Sure.

PHILIP MALLOY: So I could get my grade up,
get on the team.

COACH JAMISON: Okay.

PHILIP MALLOY: She won't let me.

COACH JAMISON: She won't let you what?

PHILIP MALLOY: Do more work.

COACH JAMISON: Well, Phil, you did one hell
of a number on her. . . .

PHILIP MALLOY: I mean, I'm not even in her class anymore. She must have kicked me out. If I could stay in her class I—

COACH JAMISON: Philip, you want my advice? I'm always telling you guys—it's what sports is all about. A rule is a rule—to get along you have to play along. Know what I'm saying?

PHILIP MALLOY: What about my running with the team?

COACH JAMISON: Look, Philip, you did a number on Miss Narwin. She's a good person. You have to be a team player. So you can't just come around now and start asking for things. It just doesn't work that way.

SLIDE: "3:30 P.M. Conversation between Margaret Narwin and Dr. Doane"

MARGARET NARWIN and DR. GERTRUDE DOANE in SR acting area. SLIDE: Office wall.

DR. DOANE: Would you like a cup of coffee?

MARGARET NARWIN: My nerves are too tight as it is.

DR. DOANE: It's astonishing. . . . I had another call from a TV reporter—

MARGARET NARWIN: You wanted to see me.

DR. DOANE: Just that some good has come out of all this. . . .

MARGARET NARWIN: That would be nice. What is it?

DR. DOANE: It concerns your application for funds for that summer refresher course, English teaching. I talked to Al Seymour and—

MARGARET NARWIN: Don't mention him to me. His statement—

DR. DOANE: But he managed to find some money, and you can take it. . . .

MARGARET NARWIN: Well, I'm very grateful.

DR. DOANE: There is only one thing. . . . Peg, he wants you to take the rest of the term off.

MARGARET NARWIN: What?

DR. DOANE: The rest of the term.

MARGARET NARWIN: But—

DR. DOANE: Take the time off, full pay, of course, and then, take that course. You'll come back fall term . . . and, well, things will be fine. It's very kind of Al.

MARGARET NARWIN: In other words, he wants me to leave.

DR. DOANE: No. No. You misunderstand. It would be an administrative leave. With pay. You'll lose no time on your pension. You could be with your sister. . . .

MARGARET NARWIN: No.

DR. DOANE: Peg, you have to see it from his, our side. . . .

MARGARET NARWIN: Aren't we on the same side?

DR. DOANE: That's not the point.

MARGARET NARWIN: What *is* the point?

DR. DOANE: Peg, Al is deeply worried about our budget.

SLIDE: "6:30 P.M. Conversation between Philip Malloy's Parents"

SUSAN and BEN MALLOY in UC acting area. SLIDE: Kitchen wall.

SUSAN MALLOY: He's very upset.

BEN MALLOY: About the telegrams?

SUSAN MALLOY: Something at school.

BEN MALLOY: The teacher again?

SUSAN MALLOY: He wouldn't say. He wouldn't talk about it.

BEN MALLOY: Strange.

SUSAN MALLOY: I almost thought he was going to start crying. Maybe you should talk to him.

BEN MALLOY: Sure.

SUSAN MALLOY: Dinner will be ready in twenty minutes. (*beat*) Hon, my sister called.

BEN MALLOY: From Conover?

SUSAN MALLOY: She said Philip could go to school in their district.

BEN MALLOY: That's absurd!

SUSAN MALLOY: Maybe it isn't. Maybe this is too much.

BEN MALLOY: Susan . . .

SUSAN MALLOY: Just a thought.

SLIDE: "8:50 P.M. From the Diary of Philip Malloy"

PHILIP MALLOY in DC acting area. He is holding his diary.

PHILIP MALLOY (*to the audience*): Things stink. And it's all so unfair. Nobody takes my side. They all think Narwin's great. Nobody pays any attention to what she did to me. Coach Jamison won't let me on the team. I hate that school.

SCENE FOUR

SLIDE: "Wednesday, April 4. 7:20 A.M. Phone conversation between Margaret Narwin and Dr. Doane"

MARGARET NARWIN and DR. GERTRUDE DOANE on opposite sides of the DC acting area.

DR. DOANE: Yes, Peg.

MARGARET NARWIN: I won't be coming in today.

DR. DOANE: Oh.

MARGARET NARWIN: I'm too exhausted.

DR. DOANE: I think that's wise.

MARGARET NARWIN: I need some time to think.

DR. DOANE: You do that. No problem here. We'll get a substitute.

SLIDE: "7:30 A.M. Conversation between Philip and His Parents at Breakfast"

PHILIP MALLOY plus SUSAN and BEN MALLOY in UC acting area. SLIDE: Kitchen wall.

PHILIP MALLOY: No way I'm going to school today.

BEN MALLOY: Why?

PHILIP MALLOY: I just won't.

SUSAN MALLOY: Philip, you must tell us. Has that teacher done something else?

PHILIP MALLOY: I'm not in her class anymore.

BEN MALLOY: But . . . look at the telegrams. Everybody says you did the right thing.

PHILIP MALLOY: I'm not going.

BEN MALLOY: Philip, you must go.

PHILIP MALLOY: I'd rather go to another school. You said there was a private school.

SUSAN MALLOY: But—

BEN MALLOY: Oh, sure! Go to a private school! The only money we've got is the money we set aside for your college.

PHILIP MALLOY: I could go to Aunt Becky's. We could move.

BEN MALLOY: That's ridiculous. Look, it's clear *something* has happened. If we don't know, how can we help you?

PHILIP MALLOY: The kids hate me!

BEN MALLOY: Why?

PHILIP MALLOY: I'm not going.

BEN MALLOY: Philip, you will go!

SLIDE: "7:40 A.M. Conversation between Philip and Ken on the Way to the School Bus"

PHILIP MALLOY and KEN BARCHET in DC acting area.

PHILIP MALLOY: What's happening?

KEN BARCHET: Nothing. What's with you? I thought maybe you weren't going to school.

PHILIP MALLOY: My folks . . .

KEN BARCHET: Did you hear what Allison and Todd were planning to do?

PHILIP MALLOY: No, what?

KEN BARCHET: They want to get a petition going to get you to say you were wrong.

PHILIP MALLOY: No way.

KEN BARCHET: And you know who gave them the idea?

PHILIP MALLOY: No.

KEN BARCHET: Coach Jamison. That's what Brian told me. I want to start another petition to get Narwin to apologize. Or we could get you to sing together. Be boss.

PHILIP MALLOY: Would you stop bugging me!

KEN BARCHET: Hey, man, can't you take a joke?

PHILIP MALLOY: Forget it.

PHILIP MALLOY exits.

KEN BARCHET: Hey! Come on, Phil. Where you going? I was just kidding!

SLIDE: "8:55 A.M. Phone conversation between Philip and His Mother"

PHILIP MALLOY in UC acting area. SUSAN MALLOY in SR acting area.

PHILIP MALLOY: Just wanted you to know I'm home.

SUSAN MALLOY: Home? Why?

PHILIP MALLOY: I told you. I'm not going to school. Not that school.

SUSAN MALLOY: Well ... stay home today. That's okay. We'll talk it out when I get home.

PHILIP MALLOY: Just don't tell Dad, will you?

SUSAN MALLOY: Okay.

SLIDE: "8:30 P.M. Ted Griffen Delivers a Speech to a Meeting of the Harrison Downtown Association"

TED GRIFFEN in DC acting area.

TED GRIFFEN (*to the audience*): That I can be a forceful, productive member of the board is clear. It was I who made public this sad story regarding the boy who was removed from class because he wanted to express his patriotism.

I was able to meet with the superintendent and discuss in a calm, rational fashion what might be done. When it became clear that the problem was not with school policy itself, but the misguided judgment of a particular teacher—a teacher out of touch with Harrison values—a solution was worked out that is equitable to all. And preserves the good name of our community. The boy is back in class, where he belongs and wants to be. The teacher in question will get a needed refresher course in our values and return to her duties next year, better able to teach.

Our community will support just these kinds

of productive compromises. And therefore I urge all of you, on April fifth, to support the school budget proposal set before the voters. It is a thoughtful budget, fiscally prudent, and I, for one, support it.

SLIDE: "10:55 P.M. Conversation between Philip Malloy's Parents"

SUSAN and BEN MALLOY in UC acting area.
SLIDE: Kitchen wall.

SUSAN MALLOY: Ben, he refuses to go back!

BEN MALLOY: I've never heard of anything so crazy. He won! But he acts as if he lost.

SUSAN MALLOY: He says he'll just wait till we're out of the house and then come home.

BEN MALLOY: Of all . . .

SUSAN MALLOY: He has to go to some school.

BEN MALLOY: Right.

SUSAN MALLOY: I'm going to call Washington Academy.

BEN MALLOY: That's his college money!

SUSAN MALLOY: Should I call my sister?

SCENE FIVE

SLIDE: "Friday, April 6. Report from the *Manchester Record* on School Elections"

JENNIFER STEWART in DC acting area.

JENNIFER STEWART (*to the audience*): Harrison School Elections. Final results, vote for school budget: six hundred forty-five in favor and seventeen hundred eighty-four against. Budget defeated. The following were elected to the Harrison School Board for three-year terms: Susan Eagleton, Ted Griffen, Gloria Haviland, Ernest Johnson, and Crawford Wright. Percentage of eligible voters casting ballots: twenty-two percent.

SCENE SIX

SLIDE: "Monday, April 9. 8:25 A.M. Conversation
between Philip and George Brookover,
Principal of Washington Academy"

*PHILIP MALLOY and GEORGE BROOK-
OVER in SR acting area. SLIDE: Office wall.*

GEORGE BROOKOVER: Philip, I just want to tell
you that we're very pleased to have you at
Washington Academy. We do know a good bit
about you. You're famous.

PHILIP MALLOY: Yes, sir.

GEORGE BROOKOVER: We like what we hear.
Anyway, we're all pretty much a family at Washington. I'm sure you'll make new friends.

PHILIP MALLOY: Yes, sir.

GEORGE BROOKOVER: You'll be in Miss Rooney's class. You'll find her a good teacher. I'm
sure you'll do just fine. Have you any interest in
sports?

PHILIP MALLOY: Track.

GEORGE BROOKOVER: Well, we don't have a track team here at Washington. There's never been enough interest. But now that you're here, maybe there can be. Your dad says you're a crackerjack runner. We do have soccer. You could do a lot of running there. Think that might interest you?

PHILIP MALLOY: I don't know.

GEORGE BROOKOVER: Okay. Let me take you on down to class now. Should be just getting under way.

SLIDE: "8:30 A.M. Miss Rooney's Homeroom Class, Washington Academy"

MISS ROONEY and PHILIP MALLOY in DC acting area. MISS ROONEY has her arm around PHILIP MALLOY'S shoulder, as if she is introducing him to the class.

MISS ROONEY (*to the audience*): Class, this is Philip Malloy, who has just joined our school. Philip, you can sit right over there. But we were about to begin our day. In fact, we usually begin by singing the national anthem. Maybe you would like to lead us in that? (*beat*) Philip? Philip, what's the matter?

The Star-Spangled Banner *begins to play.*

PHILIP MALLOY, petrified, just stands there.

PHILIP MALLOY then begins to cry.

153

PHILIP MALLOY (*finally*): I don't know the words.

The Star-Spangled Banner *gets louder as* . . .

Slides of the American flag on all three rear projection screens fade up.

PHILIP MALLOY continues crying as . . .

The national anthem and slides fade out very, very slowly until . . .

Blackout.

End of ACT TWO.

End of Play.

154